BREED FOR SUCCESS

BREED FOR SUCCESS

The Horseman's Guide to Producing Healthy Foals

By
RENÉ E. RILEY
and
HONI ROBERTS

THE LYONS PRESS
Guilford, Connecticut

The Lyons Press is an imprint of The Globe Pequot Press

The Lyons Press is an imprint of The Globe Pequot Press

10   9   8   7   6   5   4   3   2   1

Printed in the United States of America

Library of Congress Cataloging-in-Publication Data

Riley, René E.
  Breed for success : the horseman's guide to producing healthy foals / by René E. Riley & Honi Roberts.
     p. cm.
  ISBN 1-59228-604-6 (trade cloth)
  1. Horses—Breeding. 2. Horses—Parturition. 3. Veterinary obstetrics. I. Roberts, Honi. II. Title.
SF291.R55 2005
636.1'082—dc22

                                                                            2005012308

DISCLAIMER
Although every effort has been made to present scientifically correct and current information based on expert sources, readers should rely solely on their own veterinarians and equine health professionals to diagnose and treat their animals, as well as formulate a plan for breeding. Readers should be aware that all results are dependent on a variety of factors, none of which are under the control of the authors or The Lyons Press. Therefore, neither the authors nor The Lyons Press make any claim or warranty with respect to results that may be obtained from any procedures described within.

While product and/or drug brand names have occasionally been used, it has been for illustrative purposes only, and in no way constitutes an endorsement of that product, or an inference that similar products are in any way inferior. Before using any product or drug, consult with your veterinarian and follow the manufacturer's directions carefully.

Handling and breeding horses are inherently dangerous activities. Therefore, neither the authors nor The Lyons Press assume responsibility for any accident or injury resulting from a reader's interaction with horses.

We dedicate this book to the horses—past and present—
that have so generously enriched our lives. And to yours.
—René E. Riley & Honi Roberts

Contents

FOREWORD

(photo by Robert Vavra)

The clouds that had grayed the past week's skies had been blown from Andalusia. Somewhere ahead in the grove a nightingale was singing.

Of all the spring mornings spent working on the book *Equus*, this was perhaps the loveliest: the sky so freshly blue, the dew sparkling on thousands of brilliant blossoms that spread out around the olive trees.

After reading the herd, most of which were grazing, I spent the better part of an hour photographing new foals at play. At about 10:30, I decided to leave the yellow field; somewhere not far away the nightingale was still singing, and I wanted to get a closer look at him.

After I wandered about a quarter of a mile, the bird's singing suddenly stopped. As I swung around hoping to see his rust-colored body bursting in flight from one tree to another, I noticed a white mare spread out on the ground. A pair of small, blue hoof tips was just emerging from below her tail!

Almost ten minutes passed before the foal, except for his hind legs, slid from his mother. Suddenly bumped awake as he slipped onto the carpet of flowers, the foal was also shaken into consciousness by the terribly bright light around him.

(photo by Robert Vavra)

Front-lit, the scene was beautiful. But it became even more poetic when I moved around cautiously to the other side of the mare to photograph the back-lit foal. Later, walking through the olive trees, I felt completely but joyfully spent, as the nightingale sang somewhere ahead.

In the more than twenty years that have passed since then, that joy has been mine, whether I'm photographing or watching a newly born Przewalski foal, a zebra foal on the Serengeti, or a foal on my ranch in Spain. The only difference in this birth experience comes from the latter, for on my ranch, I've had some control of the foal's birth and possibly his appearance, because of the stallion I chose for the mare, and the care she is given before the birth and after it—as well as the care that is given the new foal.

For when we humans breed horses, it is essential that we do so with the knowledge of those ingredients that have the greatest chance of producing healthy, beautiful foals. This includes not only the choice of the stallion, but also the care that is given the pregnant mare and the foal before he slides from his mother, and hopefully the care they receive following that wondrous event.

So where do we acquire such knowledge? From the book by René E. Riley and my friend, Honi Roberts, that you are holding in your hands. Honi and René's lives are horses, whether they are writing about them, riding them, or caring for them. This is, then, an important document which will not only bring more beautiful and healthy foals into all of our lives, but which will also help produce the finest of mares and stallions, ensuring that future generations of horsemen will also enjoy the animals that are so important to our lives.

—Robert Vavra

(photo by Robert Vavra)

INTRODUCTION

Like every mare owner, I'd daydreamed about the foal my mare, Scecret, might produce. When she was eight years old, I seriously began to consider breeding the mare I'd fallen in love with and had brought home as a youngster. Then, as she approached her tenth year, I thought I could hear her biological clock ticking.

Although I'd loved and owned horses for most of my life, I'd never bred or planned a breeding. As a journalist, I'd consulted with breeding experts for articles, but those, however informative, were bits and pieces of the puzzle. I needed help with the entire process.

So I headed to bookstores—and found their inventory surprisingly void of a comprehensive guide to breeding horses. This void needed to be filled!

Fortunately, my good friend and one of the best equine editors and journalists in the country, René E. Riley, agreed, and we joined together to make this the most useful book on your shelf. We've interviewed veterinarians and reproductive specialists, long-time breeders, mare owners, and stallion managers. Scientific improvements in equine reproduction have been far-reaching and fast-paced in recent years, and we had a lot of ground to cover.

But in addition to the technicalities, we wanted to celebrate the joy in the journey. One must be at least a bit of a dreamer to plan a breeding or visualize a foal. And, as Sue Schembri, a top breeder of champion Appaloosa Horses notes, "It has to be a labor of love."

Love, combined with the sometimes inexplicable, always fascinating nature of horses. My friend, George Zbyszewski ("George Z" to all), told me this wonderful and true story about breeding:

"In 1977, I graduated from university in Poland, and went straight to work for a large Thoroughbred farm. It wasn't long before a young stallion with a brilliant track record arrived at the farm for his first breeding experience.

"The Jockey Club had a very strict rule that all breeding was done by natural cover. So, in the barn we had a veteran mare, in heat, awaiting him. But he showed absolutely no interest. For over two hours we tried many things, we brought the mare into and out of the room, various people in and out . . . but still no interest.

"By then, the breeding manager looked worried, I was perplexed, and no one had a solution. The groom with us, an old wizened man with much experience, spoke up. He told us the story of one celebrated stallion, famous in the days before World War II, that wouldn't mount a mare unless a live violinist played in the breeding barn.

"Well, you can imagine how hard the breeding manager and I laughed at that thought! Then we continued—still quite unsuccessfully—to interest the stallion in the task at hand.

"About an hour later, with the grim possibility of failure closing in on us, someone found a little portable radio sitting on a trunk in a far corner. We found a plug. Popular music filled the air. And a most amazing thing happened: The young stallion sniffed the mare . . . he showed interest . . . success!

"In the days, weeks, and months that followed, the breeding barn resounded with beautiful music."

Science meets the completely unscientific, absolutely mysterious element in horse breeding! Arabian breeder Christie Metz shares another spellbinding moment:

"During the birth, the entire barn is absolutely still—you can hear a piece of straw drop. Even though every stall has a horse within, it's as if we're all holding our collective breath, waiting for the great arrival.

"Then, for the first time, the mother nickers to her newborn foal. The foal answers back. And, as if on cue, every horse in the barn nickers and whinnies, and a great song arises, welcoming the baby into the world. I get chills every time. It is magic."

In *Breed for Success,* we hope to empower you with the latest technical developments on everything from embryo transfer to breeding contracts to ultrasound. But we won't forget the magic of it all. We also share breeders' unforgettable stories of trial and triumph, stories that will surely inspire you in your quest to breeding a healthy, beautiful foal. May there be joy in your journey, too.

—*Honi Roberts*

Scecret: Felicity personified. (photo by Jay Goss)

PART ONE

BEFORE YOU BREED

Quality begets quality. Varian Arabians bred Sweet Siesta V, a champion competitor, who's now producing champions, like Sacajawea V, sired by halter and Western pleasure champion, *Jullyen El Jamaal. (photo by Zita)

"INHERITANCE IGNORED"

"It's a shame," I said to Walt.
"Her conformation's filled with fault.
Her head is plain. Her neck is ewe.
Her back is long. Her tail askew.
Her shoulder straight, back at the knees;
She toes out in front, you'll notice please.
Offset cannons and splints you see.
This mare, I fear, will never be
A racing prospect, or good for show;
Brittle feet with seedy toe.

"Four years old, already lame
In both forelegs; in back the same.
Problems to worsen eventually
Because she's built inadequately.
Her hip is short. Her croup is low.
The right fore tendon's begun to bow.
She cribs, you know, and lolls her tongue—
Too many vices in a mare so young.
And when she's worked to desperation,
She wheezes with each respiration.

"Her teeth are bad. She overbites.
With other mares she always fights.
When she trots she'll weave and bobble.
Her hind end has a definite wobble.
Now melanoma in horses gray
Is very commonplace I'd say.
But these masses 'neath her tail are bad.
In a mare so young it makes me sad.
I hate to bear such tragic news:
You might as well just pull her shoes.
And stop her training as of now.
You cannot ride her anyhow."

Walt looked at me and then replied,
"The guy who sold her surely lied.
He told me that she was so great,
And I so eager, could hardly wait,
To load her up and take her home,
To pay for her, make her my own.
Well, no matter," said Walt aloud,
"She'll make a broodmare fine and proud.

"We'll breed her soon and get repaid
For the investment that I made.
I know a stallion with a fee so low
He's laid up for a year or so.
He's got navicular disease they say.
But his stud fee I guess I'll pay;
And raise a foal so this young mare
Will pay her way and earn her fare.
Don't you agree, Doc, with my plan?"
I answered him . . . I told the man:

"Like begets like. You've heard that said?
This foal you're planning, in your head,
Is good for business—mine, I mean.
Foals like this, I have seen,
Are useful to support a vet.
Because of many defects, yet
Our voice is often heard alone
Warning breeders, Do not condone
The breeding of inferior sire
To inferior mare if you desire
To produce foals to improve the breed.
Breed best to best, that's all you
need. . . .

"Like begets like. It's in the genes,
Controlled by DNA it seems.
Breed best to best, it's your only chance
For offspring that will the breed enhance."

—*Robert M. Miller, DVM*

CHAPTER ONE

TO BREED
OR NOT TO BREED

DR. ROBERT MILLER'S LIVELY, TONGUE-IN-CHEEK BALLAD makes us smile at its wit, its wonderful turn of phrase—and its truth. Who hasn't heard a similar rationale from a mare-owning acquaintance: "My mare is no good to ride or show, neither is she sound or kind-tempered—so I'll breed her."

Today, modern reproductive technology is readily available to overcome almost every physical impediment to breeding a mare. So, when idle daydreams of breeding one's horse and all its delightful possibilities turn into the very real probability of booking a stallion, conscientious breeders must ask themselves, "*Should* my mare be bred?" Not an easy question, nor is there an easy answer. But this is where we begin.

With the help of some experienced breeders, we've come up with questions for the mare owner. They're thought-provoking, pointed, philosophical, and bottom-line dollars-and-cents questions. Some will apply to everyone, some not. Read on, as they challenge you to answer the question, "To breed or not to breed?"

YOUR BREEDING GOALS

It's only during the past century that horses, historically used only for work and battle, have stepped into the role of treasured friend, partner in recreation and competition, and member of our families. There are nearly as many reasons for breeding as there are breeders. However, all would-be breeders can benefit from a thorough examination of their breeding goals.

Visualize the horse you want to breed, then strategize how to breed it. Research breeds and bloodlines. Answer these questions: Does your mare have the potential to produce the horse you desire, or should you lease a broodmare with proven capabilities? Which stallion epitomizes your ideal, and does he consistently sire offspring in his image? Can you afford to breed a foal, or would your budget better accommodate buying a quality weanling? Will you keep the foal, or if you're planning to sell him, are there ready buyers?

When you can answer these questions, you'll be on your way to breeding success and the foal of your dreams. Unlike the mare owner in Dr. Miller's poem, you'll produce a foal with a strong likelihood of being sound and hearty; a foal that's useful and has a purpose and place in the world. A foal that's the best his owner could breed.

Will my veterinarian handle breeding, pregnancy, and foaling?

Your veterinarian might've helped scores of foals into the world. There are equine veterinarians, however, who prefer not to handle pregnancies and births. Others may have limited experience with artificial insemination (AI), or the even rarer embryo transfer (ET) procedure, depending on how often these procedures are performed in your area. Ask your vet about his or her experience, how often he or she performs the procedure you'll utilize, and the success rate.

If your veterinarian either doesn't handle breeding and births or isn't experienced with the procedures your horse requires, ask him or her to refer you to a reproductive specialist nearby. Another good source for reputable equine reproductive specialists is the American College of Theriogenologists.

Other horse breeders in your area are also a valuable resource; ask them for their recommendations. Additionally, you can contact the American Association of Equine Practitioners for names of its members in your area. (For contact information on these organizations, see the resource guide.)

Is my mare a good candidate for breeding?

Once you've decided that you want to breed your favorite mare and have found a knowledgeable veterinarian to assist you, the next course of action is

Mares and foals at Crown Morgans in Hermiston, Oregon. (photo by Jay Goss)

to schedule a thorough physical examination for your mother-to-be. Pay special attention to her reproductive health. This is particularly true for *maiden mares* (those never pregnant before) and those with previous difficulties conceiving or carrying a pregnancy to term.

Now is the time to get an overall picture of her health, and ask your vet all of the questions that have been keeping you awake at night. If your mare is being bred at a stallion station, you'll need to provide a veterinarian's certificate of health before your mare arrives to be bred, so this is a great time to get one.

When your reproductive professional arrives for the examination, be prepared to relay your mare's health history, including any previous breeding and pregnancy, and any challenges experienced at that time. This will help with the current evaluation. He or she will do a rectal and vaginal exam, and will swab your mare's cervix for a bacterial culture. (See chapter 2.) If your mare has irregular estrous cycles, laboratory tests might be performed to determine her hormone levels.

After the exam is done and test results are in, you'll have a clear picture of your mare's health. Consult with your veterinarian. If your mare presents special challenges to a successful pregnancy, you'll know what you're up against and can plan accordingly. And importantly, you'll have a partner—your own veterinarian or a reproductive specialist—to offer strategy and advice, and ensure that your breeding goals are met.

Will the foal inherit my mare's strengths?

Your mare has passed her physical examination with flying colors. Next, how do you determine what your mare's bloodlines and conformation say about her breeding strengths? What will she pass on to her offspring?

"Have your mare professionally evaluated," urges horseman George Zbyszewski of George Z Training. (See chapter 7.) "Even veteran breeders can be 'barn blind,' and an unbiased opinion from someone familiar with your mare's breed and bloodlines is an excellent investment. He or she can give you valuable advice on how to breed to maximize her strengths.

"The best way to magnify your mare's strengths is to breed her to a stallion that also has those strengths. Then you'll double-up on the genetic predisposition in that area."

Justa shy guy. (photo by Heidi Nyland)

Ann Myers, owner of Western pleasure champion and leading American Quarter Horse Association sire Zips Chocolate Chip concurs. "For big-time results, determine your mare's strengths, and what discipline her bloodlines and conformation indicate she should excel in—then find a stallion with the same strengths. That's where you'll get optimum results, and have a foal that's marketable in this age of specialization."

Zips Chocolate Chip has bred scores of champion pleasure horses. "Certainly, he's had great

8

A VALUABLE LESSON

One of the horse world's great storytellers, Pat Feuerstein, shares a story about her all-time favorite mare, National Reining Horse Association champion Miss Aledo Bell. "She knew she was superior to me, because she was a horse and I was just a human. She tolerated me, and I *adored* her. A Quarter Horse, Miss Aledo Bell had halter/pleasure bloodlines, but she was too short legged to make it big-time in either event. So she became a reining horse, and did well."

One discipline's drawback may be another discipline's delight. While the mare's short stature and low center of gravity didn't particularly suit halter or Western pleasure, they were highly desirable in the fast-paced, physically demanding sport of reining.

"Later, I bred her to some of the best stallions in the industry," Feuerstein continues. "But she never produced anything comparable to herself. She wasn't bred to rein, and it showed in her offspring. Her babies were all pretty, but none of them wanted to be reining horses. She taught me a valuable lesson: When it comes to breeding, how a mare is bred is more important than what she does in the show pen."

---

success with mares that are pleasure champions themselves," Myers says. "But I try not to be prejudiced against mares without a show record. Their pedigrees will reveal a lot. I tell people, 'You don't ride the pedigree,' but it does provide clues to an unproven horse's potential talent—their family's talent—their inheritance, if you will. Is the mare's family pleasure-bred? Study the pedigree to help you select a stallion that will accentuate your mare's strengths."

My mare isn't perfect—will her offspring inherit her weaknesses?

If you have the definitive answer to this question, you win the $64,000. First, you must distinguish between *unsound characteristics* that are inherited and negatively impact a horse's health and longevity, and characteristics that are simply a *blemish*, and unacceptable for certain uses or careers. Blemishes are often temporary and not usually hereditary. And then, there are just *undesirable characteristics,* like very long ears, which are aesthetically unfortunate but never a soundness issue.

In some countries, government inspectors evaluate horses, and if they're found to be unsound, they're refused a license for breeding. Sometimes, stallions are required to be castrated to avoid any backyard "accidents." While we don't go to that extent in the United States, breeders with foresight and intelligence cull unsound horses from their breeding herd.

When you have your mare's general and reproductive health evaluated by a veterinary professional, ask him or her to identify any unsoundness in your horse's conformation. Determine whether these problems are known to be hereditary. Some common unsoundness problems that are hereditary and should give a breeder pause are: *parrot mouth* (upper teeth overlap lower teeth), *periodic ophthalmia* (cataracts that cause blindness), *severe ewe* or *wry neck* (a neck that looks like it's been put on upside down), and *umbilical hernia* (an intestinal protrusion due to the incomplete closure of the umbilical opening at birth; a veterinarian can palpate to feel the scarring that would've repaired it).

And crooked legs. Certainly, an entire book could be devoted to crooked legs. A horse's front legs support 65 percent of his weight, and are where the majority of lameness problems occur. Crooked legs—due to unsound conformation—almost guarantee future injury and lameness. For instance, the splay-footed horse, whose toes turn outward, "wings" to the inside while moving, often damaging the opposite leg. Calf-kneed horses, whose knees angle back from the front of their hooves, routinely suffer strained ligaments and carpal fractures.

If your mare has incurred lameness or injury due to her crooked legs, reconsider your breeding decision. Be totally honest: Is this a mare you want to duplicate? Love her still! And treasure her for the rest of her days. But buy or lease a *sound* mare to breed.

Blemishes don't usually eliminate a mare from breeding consideration. Normally, they're not hereditary, and may include broken teeth, saddle sores, even a sand crack in the hoof. Address blemishes with your veterinarian and, if possible, correct them before you breed. Your mare should be in the best health of her life when she begins her pregnancy.

Don Severa, co-owner of top Arabian stallion Desperado V, says that the best way to breed out a mare's undesirable characteristics is to breed her to a stallion that's strong in her weak areas. For instance, if your mare has small eyes, select a prepotent stallion that consistently stamps his offspring with big, beautiful eyes.

"Desperado kissed a lot of frogs, but I saw him stamp hundreds of offspring with his image," he says with a twinkle in his eye. "Of course, it helps if you start with a pretty, well-conformed mare. A stallion cannot be 'Mr. Magic' every time."

Severa has observed that a long back and low-set neck—undesirable characteristics that impact movement—are difficult to breed out. "I suggest looking at photographs of the mare's family. Do her dam and grandam have this characteristic? If so, it's dominant, and may be difficult to eliminate. But if she's the only one with, for example, a long back, select a prepotent stallion that routinely sires short backs." Choose wisely, and select the stallion that will minimize your mare's weaknesses.

Blastoff! (photo by Zita)

How much does the stallion add to the equation?

That depends entirely on the stallion. Never select a sire simply because he happens to be the "flavor of the month." Great breeding stallions consistently stamp their offspring with their likeness, temperament, and talent regardless of the mares they're bred to. Other stallions have considerably less impact. The only way to determine this is by researching foal crops by the stallion that's caught your eye:

- Do they share their sire's conformation and/or temperament?
- Do they excel in the same discipline? What show record have they compiled?

A reining champion, Kebra Ranch's Paint Horse stallion, Colonels Smokingun, a.k.a. "Gunner," now sires a generation of look-alike champions. (photo by Cappy Jackson)

Speak with other mare owners that have bred to the stallion. Were their foals a "chip off the old block"? While a great breeding stallion will likely have a high stud fee, this expense might easily be worth it when you consider the consistency and quality of his offspring. One breeding to him might well

---

SHEIKS AND COUNTS VYING TO BUY, OH MY!

For Drs. Jody and Karen Cruz, the 2000 Egyptian Event in Lexington, Kentucky, was a breeder's dream. They'd traveled from California to the event, the annual showcase for the Egyptian-bred Arabian, bringing their stallion Richter MH. They hadn't seriously considered selling him, the horse that best represented their third generation of careful breeding at Rancho Bulakenyo. But events would soon change their plans.

Richter won his first class, and the hearts of onlookers, too. Next was the competition for the Event's Supreme Champion Stallion. When the alabaster white stallion trotted into the ring, mane and tail flying, the crowd was electrified.

"Richter is flamboyant," Cruz says. "He's bold and full of confidence—a 14.3-hand-high horse that looks like 16 hands of pure charisma. That day, everything came together."

At one point, his trainer, Michael Byatt—who was waiting along the rail for his turn to show the stallion—told Cruz, "We should meet at the stalls after the class—there's some interest in Richter." That was an understatement. The colt that had been born the same day as one of California's largest earthquakes had shaken up some people.

Back at Richter's stall, there was a confluence of golf carts, carrying sheiks from the Middle East, American breeders, and a count from Argentina. The stallion was a white-hot property. While the owners and Jody's dad, Dr. Felino Cruz, stood back and listened, questions were asked and answered in several languages and even more accents.

"I'll never forget the moment when the count stepped forward to stand between Richter and everyone else, put his hand on the horse's neck, and said, 'Yes, he will go very well with my mares,' " Cruz says. Eventually, Richter did board a plane, and with four personal attendants at his side, flew to Argentina and Count Federico Zichy-Thyssen's mares.

And everyone lived happily ever after, of course—in this horse breeder's dream.

be worth several breedings to another, less prepotent stallion. Always choose quality over quantity.

Here's a tip: If the stud fee of a superior stallion is too steep for you, inquire about his young, up-and-coming sons. Many times, owners of top stallions will retain one or more of his sons to eventually step into their sire's illustrious shoes. Their fee will be less, but you can be assured that the stallion owner has an interest in promoting his next generation and is probably offering a fine young stallion. You'll still obtain the champion bloodlines you desire without the high fee of the family patriarch. Catch a rising star.

Can I afford it? What expenses should I expect?

Here's the reality: In nearly every instance, breeding a foal will be equally or more expensive than buying a quality weanling. After deciding to breed their mare, many first-time breeders make the mistake of thinking no further than the stallion's fee. The good news is, it's a start. The bad news is, it's just the start.

In addition to the stallion fee, expect:

- veterinarian fees for your mare's initial general health and reproductive exam, any tests, and follow-up procedures;
- fees for breeding your mare, whether live cover, artificial insemination, or embryo transfer. If you plan live cover (bringing the mare and stallion together for insemination), add the cost of transporting your mare to the stallion (see chapters 4 and 5);
- normal board and maintenance costs for the ensuing eleven-plus months. Include your farrier and any massage or alternative medical bills you normally incur, such as acupuncture or chiropractic treatment;
- ultrasound scans and other veterinarian examinations during pregnancy. If your mare has special breeding challenges, research how much this will add to your breeding bill;
- costs for making your barn and pasture foal friendly (see chapter 11);
- foaling out. If you plan to have the birth at the stallion station, a foaling station, or your reproductive specialist's facility, add board, foaling fee, and the important veterinarian's exam.

Will I keep the foal?

If you're breeding your special mare because you want her offspring to carry you over hill and dale for the next twenty years, this question is a no-brainer. Your biggest decision may be what to name the new arrival. However, it's always a good idea to consider space and accommodations for the second horse in your backyard.

First, find out whether your area has laws or zoning codes limiting the number of horses per acre. Today, this is commonplace. And, if you're adding to the number of horses kept on a small acreage, you'd be wise to consider your neighbors' possible reactions.

There's the case of one stallion owner who bred enthusiastically and very quickly found herself with twenty horses on one and a half acres. While there wasn't a rule preventing such a dense population, when her neighbors complained volubly, county officials sided with them. Citing health concerns, they demanded that she reduce her herd considerably, and bad feelings and litigation resulted.

If your property provides fresh grazing for its current equine population, will it support another horse? You might need to rotate pastures to keep the land healthy or augment your horses' diet with purchased hay. Can you accommodate the additional waste? Many owners spread their soiled bedding and manure over fallow fields or use it for fertilizer.

Do you have adequate stall or run-in shelter space for another horse? Most horses thrive on turnout. In the wild where they move freely, during inclement weather they take shelter under groves of trees, or behind huge boulders or rocky escarpments. When the rains pour down and the wind blows,

A handsome Morgan colt bred by Fire Run Farm, Snohomish, Washington.
(photo by Jay Goss)

it's best to provide your horses a refuge from the storm if your pasture lacks sheltering trees.

If I plan to sell the weanling, is there a market for him?

First, here's a dose of reality: If you think you're going to make money breeding your mare and selling the foal—think again. It's a rarity. Few small breeding operations break even. If your goal is to make money, you'd be better off moonlighting with a second job.

And face it: The market for performance weanlings is virtually nonexistent. Once your colt is two years old, the market opens up, because many youngsters are physically and mentally ready to start their under-saddle careers. But by then, you'll have invested two years of board and care into the colt, and probably the expense of some training, too. Add the cost of advertising to sell him and perhaps a trainer's commission. Now realistically compute your profit.

The market for halter horses begins at an earlier age, but unlike a performance horse that gains in value with years and experience, most halter horses peak in value before they're five years old. After that, they might be handsome has-beens. If you're going to breed a halter horse, consider what his fate will be after his show career is over.

Now, if you're still determined to breed and sell the foal, *there is some good news.* If you take the time to do your homework, you can plan for a foal to suit an existing market.

Sue Schembri and her husband own and operate Char-O-Lot Ranch in Myckka City, Florida. In 2000, the Schembris were named the Leading Breeders at the Appaloosa World Championship Show. In addition to stallions, they own or manage fifty to seventy broodmares at their facility that produce about forty foals each year.

"Breeding horses has to be a labor of love," Schembri says. "We work with many wonderful backyard breeders, and breeding is something that they really want to do—they know it's not going to be a money maker for them. A self-sustaining farm is very uncommon.

"Too many first-time breeders go into it with their eyes wide shut," Schembri continues. "Be realistic about your market! For instance, there's currently a big demand for Appaloosa hunt seat and Western pleasure horses

A beautiful newborn tries out her legs at Arabians Ltd., Waco, Texas.
(photo by Randi Clark)

to compete at the upper level. Research what mares and stallions fit the requirement and have a proven record for those disciplines. Don't breed your 14.2-hand-high mare and expect a 16.2-hand-high hunter prospect! If your goal is a hunt seat horse, make certain your mare can produce one, or purchase a broodmare that can."

Eleanor Hamilton of Eleanor's Arabians in Rogers, Minnesota, breeds and shows purebred and Half-Arabian reining and Western pleasure horses. Her stallion garnered several national reining championships in his show career, and her mares are either show winners or have strong performance bloodlines. Now, with reining's current explosion in popularity, Hamilton is enjoying an eager market for her young performance prospects, and—a rarity—she's even sold some foals in utero.

"It's vitally important for breeders to research their target market," she says. "If your interest is in reining, for instance, call breeders of champion reining stock, and ask how much their top prospects sell for, at what age, and what bloodlines are best. People are usually more than willing to talk about their horses—it's their passion—and you can get valuable information that'll help you make informed breeding decisions."

The bottom line? If you plan to sell your foal, scrutinize your target market and breed a foal that will be in demand.

Cydney Rae Cucthall meets her new best friends: Arabian broodmare and babe at Silver Maple Farm, Santa Ynez, California. (photo by Darryl Larson)

Chapter Two

Fertility & Your Mare

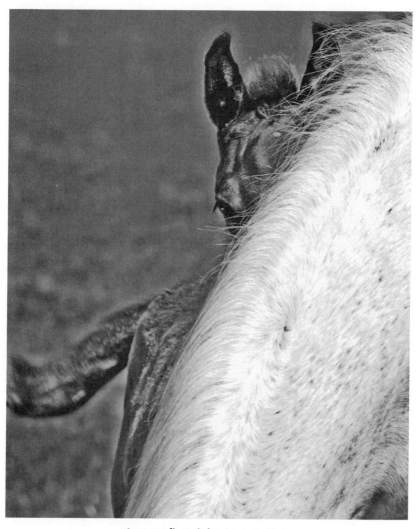

Love at first sight. (photo by Zita)

Lasting Impression

For many years it was our tradition to have Mrs. Smith, a local kindergarten teacher, bring her five- and six-year-olds to Varian Arabians in the spring for lunch and to see our broodmares with their newborn foals. One spring, more than thirty years ago now, was particularly memorable for the visiting children.

*Ostroga, one of our three foundation mares we'd imported from Poland, was heavy in foal. The children took turns putting their ears on her tummy to hear the baby. They looked at her udder to see where the baby would nurse. And the children saw the vulva, and wondered how a foal could enter the world from there. We talked about birth, and what a most amazing event it was.

The children ate their lunch, and ran and played in the pasture, neighing and galloping like horses. I showed them how to feed real horses carrots, and answered all of their questions. Then the outing was over, and the class started to board the bus to return to kindergarten.

Meanwhile, I had a closer look at *Ostroga who, without any of the usual signs of impending birth, suddenly looked for all the world like she was about to produce a baby on the spot. As I hurried *Ostroga to a foaling stall in a nearby barn, I called to Mrs. Smith that *Ostroga was going to foal, and would the children like to see the actual birth.

Twenty-five children tumbled out of the bus and raced to the barn. We had an observation room with a huge picture window attached to the stall, and the kids watched, rapt, silent—the most attentive audience you can imagine.

Afterward, I asked their help naming the foal, with the only rule that her name must begin with the same letter as the mother's name. They named the little filly Orda V—the "V" standing for Varian.

During the decades that have followed, I've run into teenagers, and now grownups with families of their own, who stop me on the street to say, "Miss Varian, I was in Mrs. Smith's kindergarten class and was there the day *Ostroga had her baby. I remember it like it was yesterday!"

—Sheila Varian, Varian Arabians, Arroyo Grande, California

THE MIRACLE OF BIRTH AS WITNESSED BY THAT GROUP OF kindergartners is a joy and wonder to behold. And the physical structures that make birth possible, which we'll discuss here, are almost as amazing as the birth itself.

Have you decided that your mare is a good candidate for breeding? Are you ready to expend the effort and cost that breeding your mare involves? Fine! But before you breed her, it's important to understand your mare's reproductive system and how she cycles throughout the year—that is, if she's healthy and cycling normally. This information in mind, you'll better understand the ways you can boost your mare's fertility, and how you can manage the timing of conception and birth, if such management is important to you.

In this chapter, we'll explain all of this with the help of Khris Crowe, DVM, MS, PC, an equine-reproduction specialist based at the Babcock Ranch in Gainesville, Texas.

FERTILITY FACTS

Before we can go into how you can manage fertility in your mare, we'll need to discuss a mare's reproductive system and cycles. Use this section as a reference, especially if you find your mare has a problem conceiving and/or if you'd like to manage her cycles to control the timing of conception and birth.

The Reproductive System

Now, here's a brief rundown of a healthy mare's reproductive anatomy and the role of each organ so you can better comprehend her cycles and fertility.

A healthy mare's reproductive tract consists of nine basic components. Here's a list of those organs and their functions, from the outside in.

- *Vulva:* The most external portion of the mare's genitalia that represents the opening into her reproductive tract.
- *Clitoris:* Located just inside the vulva, the mare's clitoris is analogous to the stallion's penis.
- *Vestibule:* A short, tube-like cavity that links the vulva and vagina.
- *Vagina:* The birth canal.

- *Cervix:* The narrow structure that connects the vagina and uterus. The cervix closes tightly to protect the uterus from contamination when she's out of heat (which we'll discuss in a minute) and during pregnancy.
- *Uterus:* The mare's hollow reproductive organ, in which the fetus will develop.
- *Uterine body:* The part of the uterus between the uterine horns (below) and the cervix. The uterine body nourishes a developing fetus during pregnancy.
- *Uterine horns:* The two upper projections in the Y-shaped uterus that connect the oviduct to the uterus.
- *Oviduct:* The egg's passageway; also called the fallopian tube.
- *Ovaries:* Reproductive glands that produce eggs for fertilization. A mare normally will have a left and right ovary.

The Reproductive Cycle

Mares are *seasonally polyestrous,* meaning they have normal estrous cycles only part of the year, usually from early spring through late fall. Peak months are May, June, and July. Transitional periods are September, October, February, and March. The estrous season is followed by a period of *anestrus,* during which mares don't experience estrous cycles. We'll focus on the mare's estrous cycle, as it's during this cycle that you'll need to breed your mare.

The term *estrous cycle* describes the mare's entire reproductive cycle, which lasts an average of twenty-one to twenty-two days. This cycle can be broken into two stages: *estrus,* in which she's "in heat" and receptive to the stallion; and *diestrus,* in which she's out of heat and likely to fight off a stallion's advances. Estrus lasts about five to six days; diestrus lasts the remainder of the time.

During estrus, several *follicles* develop on the mare's ovaries. A follicle is a fluid-filled sac that contains the *ovum* (egg), which produces *estrogen* (a reproductive hormone). A mare with a developing follicle and under the influence of estrogen will lift her tail, urinate, and expose her clitoris in a stallion's presence to show signs of heat. During this time, she'll likely allow a stallion to mount and breed her.

At the end of estrus, the *primary* (largest) follicle *ovulates*—that is, ruptures and releases an egg. The ruptured follicle fills with blood and develops

All legs at Varian Arabians. (photo by Zita)

a cellular structure called a *corpus luteum* (CL). This CL produces *progesterone*, the hormone necessary to maintain pregnancy. The egg is collected by *fimbriae* (small, finger-like projections) at the end of the oviduct.

LIGHT BREEDING

Mares throughout the world differ in their seasonal breeding patterns. A mare found close to the equator has relatively normal cycles throughout most of the year due to the regular, long daylight hours. A mare closer to the North or South Pole has a relatively short breeding season, because she experiences shorter daylight periods.

The breeding season in the northern hemisphere is the opposite of the season in the southern hemisphere, because each hemisphere receives opposite lengths of daylight exposure. As you know, when it's summer here in the United States, it's winter in Australia. A mare in the northern hemisphere is most fertile from February to June, while a mare in the southern hemisphere is most fertile from September to January.

If the mare has been bred, sperm wait inside the oviduct for the egg to arrive for fertilization. If the mare isn't bred, or is bred but doesn't become pregnant, she'll shed the egg and remain in diestrus until it's time for her to develop follicles—and the process is repeated. If a pregnancy develops, the mare won't show heat until after foaling.

Light, not temperature, affects a mare's breeding cycles. Increased daylight hours cause your mare to begin having normal estrous cycles, and decreased daylight hours cause her fertility to decline, ultimately leading to an anestrous period. That's why light manipulation, discussed later in this chapter, plays such an important role when managing your mare's breeding season.

Is Your Mare Ready?

The ideal broodmare is three to twelve years old and in good body condition. (Although this is considered the prime age window, note that a mare younger than three years old can successfully produce embryos, and some mares into their twenties produce healthy foals.)

She has full, symmetrical, tightly closing labia that are perpendicular to the ground and don't tilt or tip. Her vagina is healthy and free of urine or fecal contamination, and is roughly perpendicular to her backbone, as opposed to tipping toward her abdomen. Her cervix is healthy and can fully close and open during estrous cycles. Her uterus is free from fluid and cysts. She has two normal, walnut-sized ovaries that actively produce and ovulate follicles.

How closely does your mare match the ideal? A breeding-soundness evaluation (BSE), performed by a veterinarian, will help you evaluate her reproductive health and identify any obstacles you might need to address before you breed her. (See page 26.)

Fertility Boosters

By boosting your mare's fertility, you'll give her the best possible chance of producing a healthy foal. Following are five fertility boosters, why they're important, and how to implement each one.

Easy to see the resemblance between this exquisite Varian Arabians mare and her daughter. (photo by Zita)

THE BREEDING-SOUNDNESS EVALUATION

A breeding-soundness evaluation (BSE) will help you evaluate whether your mare will easily conceive or whether she might be a problem mare. This evaluation can be especially helpful if your mare has never been bred before, and/or you're aware that she's had problems conceiving in the past. This evaluation is also recommended as part of the pre-purchase examination on a mare you plan to use for breeding.

Any problems identified during the BSE must be dealt with immediately to preserve your mare's reproductive health and increase the odds of successful breeding. (For details on reproductive challenges, see chapter 6.)

Note that the BSE is best performed while your mare (or broodmare prospect) is in heat, as the attending veterinarian will be able to identify problems not present when your mare is out of heat. The evaluation generally includes the following elements:

External reproductive-conformation evaluation. You can learn a lot about a mare simply by lifting her tail. Abnormal conformation, such as a tipped vulva, a vulva that doesn't seal well, a low pelvic bone, or a pulled-forward rectum all can lead to breeding problems, as they tend to allow contaminants into the reproductive tract.

Rectal examination. The rectal exam identifies abnormal ovaries—or even a lack of ovaries, if the mare has had them removed (that is, an *ovariectomy* has been performed). This exam also identifies ovarian tumors.

Ultrasound scan. An ultrasound scan evaluates your mare's entire reproductive tract. This tool allows a veterinarian to examine your mare's uterine fluid and its consistency, which offer important clues as to her uterine health. Clear fluid appears black on the ultrasound screen, while fluid with particulate matter, such as pus, is very gray. Large quantities of fluid or fluid containing particulate matter can signify infection.

Ultrasound scans also identify uterine cysts, which can pose concerns depending upon their size and location. Small cysts generally aren't problematic. An ultrasound scan of the ovaries identifies any abnormalities and determines the stage of your mare's estrous cycle.

Uterine cytology. In this test, a fluid sample recovered from your mare's uterus is smeared on a slide and stained to identify inflammation and infection.

THE BREEDING-SOUNDNESS EVALUATION (continued)

Uterine culture. In this test, your mare's uterus is swabbed, and that sample is examined for bacteria and sensitivity to antibiotics to identify a course of treatment, if necessary.

Endometrial biopsy. In this test, tissue removed from your mare's uterus is preserved and cross-sectioned to assess the health of the uterine lining. The tissue is then graded. (See chapter 6.)

Cervical examination. This exam identifies cervical scarring and tearing that can hinder the breeding process.

—*Jill (Thayer) Cook, DVM*

Fertility booster #1: Record keeping.

Why it's important: These records make it easier to time optimal breeding, because you'll get a better feel of the timing of your mare's particular heat cycles, and the signs of heat she exhibits.

What you'll do: As soon as you know you want to breed your mare, start keeping notes. Record when her first heat cycle of the year occurs, the signs of heat she exhibits, and how long she's in heat. Also keep track of any health problems she's had and treatments she's received, as well as any hormone therapies your veterinarian might've prescribed. Once she's bred, note the length of her gestation, because she'll probably follow the same schedule each time she's bred.

Fertility booster #2: Teasing.

Why it's important: Veterinarians vary in how they think teasing should be used in a breeding program. Dr. Crowe is a big proponent of teasing breeding mares. Research suggests that exposing your mare to a stallion and eliciting all the physical signs of heat is physically beneficial. Further, teasing allows you to identify your mare's heat cycle.

What you'll do: You'll expose your mare to a teasing stallion for two to five minutes every other day during the breeding season. Caveat: Only an experienced handler using a well-trained stallion should perform the teasing process, as it can be dangerous to both horse and human. Here's why: During teasing, the stallion is allowed to interact with the mare, but he doesn't

Trotting into your heart: a dynamic Morgan colt bred by Fire Run Farm.
(photo by Jay Goss)

receive a sexual release, which can lead to aggressive behavior. Also, a mare that's not in heat—and not receptive to a stallion's advances—might respond negatively. She can do anything from walking away with her ears pinned to trying to go through the stall door.

Fertility booster #3: Timing of insemination.

Why it's important: You need to know when she's ovulating (in that short window of twenty-four to forty-eight hours before she goes out of heat), so you can breed her at just the right time—either by live cover or via artificial insemination.

What you'll do: To identify signs of heat, you'll tease your mare. During heat, you'll schedule an appointment with your veterinarian. He or she will perform an ultrasound scan at least every forty-eight hours, which will show uterine folds and swelling (an internal sign of estrus) and the follicle on the

Everything is new, everything is interesting to foals at Varian Arabians.
(photo by Zita)

FIND A VETERINARIAN

To find a reputable reproductive veterinarian in your area, contact the American College of Theriogenologists. Or, contact the American Association of Equine Practitioners. (For contact information on these organizations, see the resource guide.)

Also, ask other breeders in your area whom they use. If there's a large breeding facility in your area, it's a good bet they use an experienced breeding veterinarian.

Ask a prospective veterinarian about his or her experience with breeding mares and what services the practice provides. You want to find a veterinarian who breeds many mares as opposed to one who handles the breeding process only occasionally. An experienced veterinarian keeps up to date on the latest technologies and techniques. If your regular veterinarian doesn't handle breeding mares, he or she might recommend a more suitable practitioner for the process.

---

ovary. Once the primary follicle measures about one and one half inches in diameter (thirty-eight millimeters), it's almost ready to ovulate. This allows you to more closely pinpoint when to breed your mare.

You want to inseminate your mare forty-eight hours prior to ovulation if you're using fresh semen or live cover; twelve to twenty-four hours prior to ovulation if you're using cooled or frozen semen. (See chapter 4.)

Your vet will continue to perform ultrasound scans on your mare to make sure the primary follicle has ruptured. If it hasn't ruptured within forty-eight hours of breeding, you'll need to inseminate your mare again, as by then the sperm cells will have lost their fertility.

If you don't have access to ultrasound, tease your mare every day to pinpoint when she's receptive to the stallion and in heat. Begin breeding her on the third day of her cycle, and then every other day until she goes out of heat. (You'll know she's out of heat when she doesn't respond to the stallion.)

Fertility booster #4: Light management.

Why it's important: Light plays a major role in your mare's estrous cycles. In a natural setting, a mare is designed to come into heat in the late spring to early summer, be bred by a stallion, and produce a foal in the spring when the weather is warming and forage is abundant. In the fall, a mare becomes progressively less fertile.

What you'll do: You'll increase your mare's exposure to light to about sixteen hours per day to make her become fertile earlier in the year. This might be important to you if you'd like an early season foal that will later have the advantage of maturity in competition, since all horses are considered another year older on January 1, regardless of the month in which they were actually born.

A FEBRUARY FOAL

A mare owner in Louisiana arranged to have his twelve-year-old Quarter Horse mare bred via cooled shipped semen from a stallion in California. He wanted an early February foal the following year. He provided the mare sixteen hours of light per day by turning her out in the pasture all day, and leaving her under artificial light in the barn every night.

In mid-February, the owner began teasing the mare with a young stallion. Although the mare had shown obvious signs of heat the previous year—lifting her tail, bracing her back, and urinating—she showed no signs of heat now that the owner was trying to have her bred.

During the first week of March, the owner arranged for his veterinarian to examine the mare to find out why she wasn't coming into heat. An ultrasound scan of her left ovary showed the presence of an unfertilized corpus luteum (CL) that was preventing heat. The veterinarian gave the mare a prostaglandin injection, which destroyed the CL.

Five days later, the mare showed signs of heat. On the third day of heat, the veterinarian returned to perform an ultrasound exam and found a mature follicle on the mare's left ovary. The owner arranged for semen to be shipped the next day and scheduled an HCG injection to cause ovulation to coincide with the arrival of the semen. The mare was inseminated and became pregnant. Her foal arrived the second week of February—just as the owner wanted.

—*Khris Crowe, DVM, MS, PC*

A charming Quarter Horse foal. (photo by Heidi Nyland)

To manipulate your mare's cycle so she'll foal just after January 1, begin providing light supplementation between November 15 and December 1. She'll be ready for breeding around mid- to late-February, assuming all other conditions are normal.

To increase light exposure to sixteen hours per day, you can turn your mare out during daylight hours, then bring her into a stall at dusk under artificial light. For a twelve by-twelve-foot stall, a 200-watt light bulb will be sufficient. Make sure you can read a newspaper with that light in all corners of your mare's stall, and close all the exterior windows so she can't hang her head in the dark. Set the bulb on a timer so that she receives enough light to total sixteen hours per day.

Note: Don't keep your mare under lights year round. Doing so can seriously alter her seasonal responses to the point that she'll be fertile in November and December and go into anestrus during prime breeding months.

Fertility booster #5: Hormone therapy.

Why it's important: There are three commonly used supplemental hormones used in equine reproduction; each can be important in its own way.

What you'll do: If your veterinarian determines hormone therapy might be beneficial for your mare, you'll work with him or her on the best program. There are three types of hormones commonly used in equine reproduction; here's a rundown of each one.

Prostaglandin (brand names, Lutalyse and Estrumate).

If your mare is pregnant, she'll have a progesterone-producing CL, which is, of course, your goal. However, if she's not pregnant and the CL stays on the ovary, she won't come back into heat for her next cycle, which can delay the breeding process. Administering prostaglandin will destroy the CL and bring her into heat within three to five days. (Note: If you're mare *is* pregnant, prostaglandin will cause her to spontaneously abort the pregnancy.)

Human chorionic gonadatropin (HCG).

This hormone—derived from the urine of pregnant women—is given when the mare has folds in her uterus and a one-and-a-half-inch-diameter (thirty-eight millimeter) follicle. As it'll cause the follicle to ovulate within thirty-six hours, HCG is most useful for timing your mare to ovulate to coincide with the arrival of shipped cooled or frozen semen.

Synthetic progesterone (brand name, Regumate).

This hormone is actually used to prevent estrus to, for example, improve a mare's mood and modify her behavior during competition. However, the hormone can be helpful in breeding, as your mare will start to cycle two to four days after she's taken off it. Knowing this can help you plan ahead when timing insemination. Synthetic progesterone is also used to maintain pregnancy in problem mares.

Note: Again, use hormone therapy only on the advice of your veterinarian. Improper hormone treatment can seriously alter your mare's estrous cycles, and can have undesirable side effects. For example, prostaglandin can cause a mare to sweat profusely, experience severe muscle relaxation, and/or have abdominal muscle contractions that look like stomach crunches. HCG, if used too often, can cause a mare to become resistant to its effects.

Synthetic progesterone allows the spread of any existing uterine infection or contamination, because it closes the cervix and depresses a mare's immune system to keep it from attacking the developing fetus.

In sync! Varian champion, Amazing Grace V, with daughter, Amelia Jullyen V.
(photo by Zita)

CHAPTER THREE

PRE-BREEDING MARE CARE

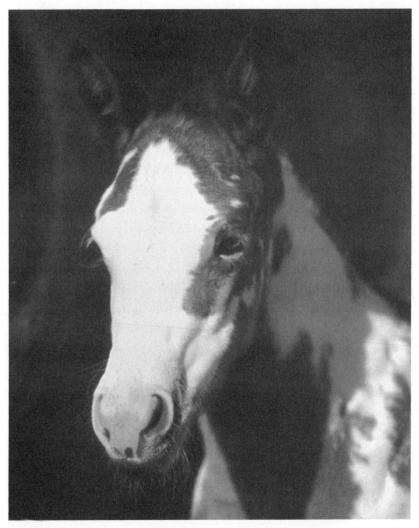

A colorful Paint Horse youngster. (photo courtesy of the American Paint Horse Association)

A Breeder's Dream

I've bred horses for most of my life, and owned a lot of broodmares—there were sixty-five in my pasture at one time. But it was a loud overo mare we called Molly who really established me in the Paint Horse business.

Her registered name was Pocahontas, and I first saw her when she had a young colt at her side. I knew immediately I'd like to have her and tried to buy her then, but they wouldn't sell. Her owner planned to give the colt to his wife. Fortunately for me, the colt turned out to be more horse than she wanted, so one day, he brought the mare and that colt, Wahoo King, to my farm. He wanted to trade them both for a top King Ranch show gelding I had. I told him, "You've just made a trade."

At first, my friends thought I was crazy—but I cannot tell you how good that mare was to us! She was a broodmare supreme, producing a colt every year. Never a filly, although she'd had a filly before I bought her. Eventually I tracked down that filly, Shady Lane, and bought her, too.

Some folks might've complained about all the colts, but when they were like Wahoo King, a legendary roping horse in the 1960s, J Bar Junior, a national halter champion, C Note, and more—I was more than pleased!

Molly was real pretty with her loud coloring, and she bred and settled easily. She was a great mother, and produced milk like a Holstein cow—just what growing colts need. Often, we bred her to our stallion, Mister Jay Bar, five-time national halter and roping champion. She was one of the few horses I've owned in my life that I never even considered selling. We kept her until cancer took her from us.

Today, when people talk about Pocahontas, they describe her as a great American Paint Horse Association foundation mare, and a legend. To us, she was the sweet mare who preferred to stay at the barn to be by people, instead of out in the pasture. Molly, who put me on the map in the breeding business.

—Junior Robertson, cofounder of the APHA, Waurika, Oklahoma

JUNIOR ROBERTSON TREASURED HIS OUTSTANDING PAINT Horse mare, Molly. Her longevity as a proven broodmare speaks volumes about the horseman's care and concern for her health and well-being. Your mare's overall pre-breeding health program—and everything that goes along with it—affects how well she conceives, maintains the pregnancy, and delivers her foal. Your mare's pre-pregnancy health even affects the foal after it's born.

Although most of your pre-breeding health program will simply include the elements that make up sound management of any horse, there are a few differences. For one, you'll need to be extra careful that you follow the program explicitly, without taking any shortcuts. Such shortcuts will only result in greater cost and time on your part to produce a foal.

Jill (Thayer) Cook, DVM, focuses her practice on equine reproduction at Royal Vista Equine, Inc., in Fort Collins, Colorado, which is owned by Dr. Cook and her husband, Vaughn. At the facility, Dr. Cook stands five stallions, and provides embryo-transfer and artificial-insemination services for mare owners.

Here, Dr. Cook discusses the top management areas to address in your mare's pre-breeding health program. These areas include stress, vaccinations, deworming, nutrition, weight, exercise, dental health, and hoof care/lameness. She also tells you three things you *shouldn't* do prior to breeding your mare.

MARE MANAGEMENT

Management area #1: Stress.

Why it's important: Stress can lead to irregular or unpredictable cycles, and can even cause your mare to stop cycling altogether. This, of course, can put a serious crimp in your breeding program. A stressful event can also cause other physiological changes, such as weight loss, that also affect fertility, as we'll discuss later in this chapter.

Proven program: First, become aware of the stressors that might be affecting your mare—both physical (internal) and psychological (external). Physical causes of stress include poor health, chronic health conditions (such as chronic lameness), poor dental health, and poor nutrition. Psychological causes of stress include being at the bottom of the herd's pecking order, being away from herdmates or a barn buddy, and even weather extremes.

Then, minimize or eliminate these stressors. Signs of stress include uneasiness, sweating, weight loss, or decreased water and feed intake. Furthermore, if she's stressed she might have a dull coat or not keep up with her herdmates. "Every situation is different, so stress management isn't black or white," says Dr. Cook. For instance, if you need to haul your mare to a breeding farm, watch to see whether she settles right in, or is still nervous after a day or two. If she seems stressed out, do whatever you can to reduce her stress. Slowly change her diet to what she'll be fed at the farm. If she's uncomfortable trailering, make a few practice trips to help her relax in the trailer. If allowed, get her a companion animal, such as a goat or Miniature Horse. Ask those caring for your mare during the breeding process to help you get her settled into her new environment as quickly as possible.

Management area #2: Vaccinations.

Why it's important: Most veterinarians advise against vaccinating your mare during her first forty-five to ninety days of pregnancy (see chapter 9), so pre-

Fleur and Denini: A barn cat can make a fine companion for your mare.
(photo by honi)

breeding vaccinations will help protect her against infectious diseases during that important time. This is especially important if you take your mare to a breeding farm and/or foaling station, where she'll be exposed to unfamiliar horses that might carry disease.

Proven program: Follow the advice of your veterinarian. He or she will likely vaccinate your mare against tetanus, equine encephalitis (also known as sleeping sickness; depending on where you live, this vaccination will include the Western equine, Eastern equine, and/or Venezuelan equine varieties), equine influenza, and equine viral rhinopneumonitis. Depending on where you live, your vet will also give your mare vaccinations for equine viral arteritis (EVA), West Nile virus; equine monocytic erhlichiosis (Potomac horse fever), strangles, and rabies.

Note that most vaccines must be given twice for optimal protection the first time your mare is vaccinated or if her vaccination history isn't known. The series includes one initial vaccination followed by a booster three to four weeks later. Your veterinarian will likely administer the initial vaccination seven to eight weeks prior to breeding, and give the booster vaccination at least two to three weeks before your mare is bred or goes to the breeding farm. Yearly boosters should be given two to three weeks prior to breeding.

Management area #3: Deworming.

Why it's important: Your mare should be as free as possible from internal parasites for the sake of her own health, and that of her future foal. Parasites steal nutrition from your mare and can cause *colic* (abdominal pain caused by digestive disorder).

Proven program: Follow the advice of your veterinarian. He or she will likely recommend that you deworm your mare thirty days prior to breeding to make sure your mare is able to overcome any related stress before she's bred.

Tip: If you feed your mare a daily dewormer and she'll be bred away from home, you can have the breeding farm continue the daily dewormer or take her off the product. If you do the latter, administer a paste dewormer to purge her system before resuming the daily product.

Management area #4: Nutrition.

Why it's important: Quality nutrition plays a major role in successful breeding. Weight issues (which we'll discuss in a minute) and mineral imbalances can adversely affect conception and fetal development.

Proven program: The majority of your mare's diet should come from forage—grass hay or alfalfa. Her body is designed to eat and digest forage. Base the amount of forage you feed your mare on her body condition. If she needs to gain weight, offer her high-quality alfalfa and grain, which contain calories and nutrition. If she needs to lose weight, offer her grass hay, which has fewer calories.

Have your hay tested by your local extension service or feed company to see if it's deficient in any minerals, and to evaluate its value for protein and digestibility. The calcium-to-phosphorous ratio is extremely important for broodmares, because it affects the developing foal, so make sure it's also sufficient in your mare's pre-breeding diet. A sufficient ratio is usually 2:1 to 3:1. Generally speaking, horses fed grass hay require calcium supplementation and those fed alfalfa need extra phosphorous.

Mutual grooming provides social interaction, and is an important stress release for herd animals. (photo by honi)

You might be tempted to supplement your mare's diet with trace minerals. Trace minerals are vital to her health, but she might be getting all she needs in her forage. (You'll know after you have your forage tested.) If you feel you need to add mineral supplements, stick with the basics. Oversupplementation can prevent some minerals from being absorbed and can actually become toxic. (For details, consult with your veterinarian.)

Tip: Provide any trace-mineral, calcium-phosphorous, and salt blocks intended for equine use—not those intended for other livestock, which have a different mineral composition.

Of course, give your mare unlimited access to a salt/mineral block and clean water.

Management area #5: Weight.

Why it's important: A very thin mare won't cycle well, especially early in the year. A very fat or obese mare also doesn't cycle well—in fact, an obese mare is the worst performer, reproductively speaking, in every category. Weight issues also affect pregnancy. (See chapter 10.)

Proven program. Ideally, your mare should have a score of 5 or 6 on the Henneke Body-Condition Index. (See page 42.) That means she's of a moderate weight and in good condition. Simply continue a sound maintenance diet, discussed earlier.

If your mare is closer to a 4, or moderately thin, and gaining weight going into the breeding season, she shouldn't experience any adverse affects during breeding. In fact, some veterinarians and breeding professionals believe it's good for a mare to be "on the gain" as she enters the breeding season. This is based on the belief that a mare should be in the same natural condition she'd be in after a winter of poor forage in the wild. Other veterinarians feel that a mare should be in optimal health when going into breeding season.

Still, see your veterinarian for how to bring your underweight mare up to an optimal weight prior to breeding her. Generally, make sure to feed your mare high-quality forage. Add grain to supplement her caloric intake. Add one-fourth to one-half cup of vegetable oil on top of her feed for extra fat.

If your mare is overweight, note that weight loss during breeding can affect fertility, so make any changes in your mare's diet and exercise regimen *now*, well before she's bred. If your mare has a score of 8 or 9 on the

Henneke Body-Condition Index, start her weight-loss program at least six months before breeding season begins. A severely obese mare can take even longer to lose weight and attain good pregnancy shape. Ask your veterinarian to evaluate your mare and recommend a weight-loss program.

Generally, if your mare is simply an *easy keeper* (that is, keeps weight on without trouble), you'll need to reduce her feed or provide low-calorie forage, such as grass hay rather than alfalfa. Turn her out on dry pasture, and increase her exercise (which we'll discuss in a minute).

HENNEKE BODY-CONDITION INDEX

Don R. Henneke, PhD, developed the Henneke body-condition scoring system to evaluate a horse's condition, regardless of breed, body type, size, sex, or age. The evaluation is based on both visual and palpable fat throughout the horse's body. The chart offers a score from 1 to 9 (poor to extremely fat) and provides a standardized way to communicate a horse's condition.

To evaluate your mare's condition, visually evaluate and *palpate* (firmly run your fingertips over) six areas: neck, withers, shoulder, ribs, loin, and tailhead. Assign a score of 1 to 9 to each area evaluated, according to how thin or fat, and divide the total of those numbers by 6.

Tip: Don't let a full winter coat fool you—you must feel the areas in order to identify fat. A mare nearing foaling or a broodmare might look fat due to stretched abdominal muscles, but it's imperative that you evaluate the fat over her back to determine whether she's overweight.

Use the scoring system when monitoring an under- or overweight mare's progress toward ideal condition. Evaluate her condition every six weeks, noting any feed changes along the way.

HENNEKE BODY-CONDITION SCORING CHART

Score Body-Condition Description

1 *Poor;* bone structure easily noticeable in the neck, withers, shoulder, and vertebrae; ribs prominently protrude; tailhead stands out.
2 *Very thin;* bone structure faintly noticeable in the neck, withers and shoulder; prominent ribs; slight amount of fat along the back, at the *spinous processes* (points of the vertebrae); tailhead stands out.

HENNEKE BODY-CONDITION SCORING CHART (CONTINUED)

3 *Thin*; neck, withers, and shoulder accentuated; slight fat over ribs, but ribs are easily seen; prominent tailhead, but individual vertebrae aren't easily seen.

4 *Moderately thin*; neck, withers, and shoulder not obviously thin; fat felt at tailhead.

5 *Moderate* (ideal); neck and shoulder blend smoothly into the body; rounded withers; ribs not easily seen, but felt; slightly spongy tailhead fat.

6 *Moderately fleshy*; fat beginning to accumulate at the neck, withers, and behind the shoulder; slight crease down back; ribs feel slightly spongy; tailhead fat is spongy.

7 *Fleshy*; fat easily felt along the neck and withers, and behind the shoulder; individual ribs can be felt with pressure, but noticeable fat between ribs; tailhead fat is soft.

8 *Fat*; noticeably thick neck; withers filled with fat; area behind the shoulder is flush with body; difficult to feel ribs; very soft tailhead.

9 *Extremely fat*; bulging fat at the neck, withers, and shoulder; patchy fat over ribs; crease down the back; inner thighs and flanks filled with fat.

Turnout and exercise helps keep your broodmare healthy. (photo by honi)

Management area #6: Exercise.

Why it's important: Exercise helps to maintain your mare's muscle tone and improves circulation. It can even help reduce risk of colic and other health problems. If you don't exercise your mare, she'll likely gain weight, which can harm her chances of becoming pregnant. Also, if your mare is used to exercise, she'll likely become stressed if she's cooped up in a stall all day.

Proven program: Free exercise—such as turnout in a pasture or large paddock—is ideal. Moderate riding is also excellent for a mare entering the breeding season. If your mare is accustomed to performing and doesn't become stressed by competition, you can keep showing her. However, don't put her under unusually high levels of performance stress immediately prior to breeding. If she's not acclimated to hauling and competing, don't expect her to do so as she enters the breeding season.

Avoid any sudden increase in exercise levels. Switching to a heavy workout just before breeding can stress your mare, especially if she isn't fit to begin with. And if she loses a lot of weight, she won't be at her breeding best.

Management area #7: Dental health.

Why it's important: Good dental health allows your mare to eat comfortably and extract optimal nutrition from her feed. If she suffers from, for instance, broken teeth or infected gums, she won't be able to chew her food properly. This can lead to poor nutrition, weight loss, and colic, all of which can negatively affect the breeding process.

Proven program: Note that when your mare becomes pregnant, she can't have any dental work—the heavy sedation and bacterial exposure can compromise fetal health. So have your mare's teeth examined just before you breed her and just after she foals. When your mare is *open* (not pregnant), have her teeth examined once or twice yearly.

Management area #8: Hoof care/lameness.

Why it's important: A mare with poor feet or suffering from chronic hoof problems is uncomfortable, which can cause stress. Your mare doesn't need to be sound enough to ride in order to be a broodmare. If she's a little sore and can be made comfortable in her surroundings, her pain shouldn't be a

(photo by honi)

problem. However, if it's not managed, she'll encounter problems at breeding time. If ignored, minor foot problems can lead to more severe issues, such as sole abscesses, painful hoof cracks, and overall foot pain.

Proven program: Your mare doesn't need perfectly beautiful feet when you breed her; she doesn't even need to wear shoes. Have her feet trimmed—but not too short—and address any lameness problems, whether through corrective shoeing, medication, or other methods.

Should you medicate your lame mare to manage pain prior to breeding? There's some controversy surrounding this issue. For example, studies support that too much nonsteroidal anti-inflammatory medication in a mare's system decreases fluid clearance from the uterus, which can lead to poor conception. But if your mare is in pain, she won't cycle or conceive well, either. Discuss this issue with your veterinarian. Weigh the benefits and costs of her being comfortable versus a quick conception. This decision must be made on an individual basis, depending upon your mare's condition and history.

WHAT *NOT* TO DO

Here are three things you *shouldn't* do during the pre-breeding period in order to maximize the chance of obtaining a successful pregnancy.

Don't expect too much from an aged maiden mare.

A mare bred for the first time when she's more than twelve years old is more difficult to breed than a mare bred once earlier in life. If you plan to breed your mare later in her life, it's best to have her carry a foal at a younger age, proceed with her career, then use her as a broodmare.

Don't keep your mare under lights year round.

A light program can be useful to manipulate your mare's breeding cycle. (See chapter 2.) However, using lights year round makes it very difficult to breed her at a predetermined time. At some point, her body has to shut down into an anestrous cycle; if she's under lights all the time, you won't know when her body will go into that phase. She might go into an anestrous cycle right when she arrives at the breeding farm. Once you lose control over her cycle, it can take sixty to ninety days for her to return to a normal cycle.

Ideally, discontinue your mare's light program in the early fall so she'll go into a natural anestrus. Then return her to lights in December, and she'll be ready to breed early in the season.

To show how lights can be incorrectly used, Dr. Cook offers this case study. "A competitive English pleasure show mare was brought to our veterinary clinic in Fort Collins, Colorado, for breeding," she says. "She'd been on a year-round light program and kept in a heated barn. The mare went into an anestrous cycle upon arrival, possibly triggered by moving her from her normal environment and the associated stress. That prolonged the breeding process.

"I put the mare back under lights, blanketed the mare, supplemented her feed with vegetable oil, and used hormonal therapy to instigate a normal cycle," continues Dr. Cook. "The process took nearly ninety days, which led

---

MANAGING HEAT

Heat and its associated behavior are sometimes a curse to competitive/active horsepeople—but are actually a blessing to a breeder. You want your mare to show strong signs of heat, as outlined here. To you, this means your mare is cycling normally and any outward signs of heat can help you monitor her cycles.

On the other hand, you're still riding and perhaps showing your mare in the months leading up to breeding. So you, like most mare owners, need a way to manage the sometimes aggravating behavior that accompanies heat.

Normal signs of heat include frequent urination; *winking* (tail raised, vulva contracting); squealing and kicking; backing up to other horses; an increased interest in other horses; a lack of normal sensitivity and response to rider cues; and a lack of focus.

Training can improve your mare's behavior, but much of this natural behavior requires hormone therapy to control it. If you think your mare might be a candidate for hormone therapy, discuss the options with your veterinarian.

to increased expense for the owner and lost time in the mare's competitive career. Also, the mare owner's goal of having an early foal wasn't met."

Don't overuse hormone therapy.

Sometimes, there's a need for hormone therapy, such as to keep your mare from having behavioral problems during training or showing. But don't continually administer hormones if you intend to breed her in the future. Her body needs a break. Long-term use of hormones can alter her natural hormonal pattern and make breeding difficult. The shorter the use, the better.

Also, use caution when administering hormones to prepubescent fillies (those twelve to eighteen months old). Hormonal manipulation at that point can cause long-term damage. Wait until the filly reaches sexual maturity to use hormonal therapy.

Put the bloom on your broodmare with fresh air, green grass, and sunshine. (photo by honi)

CHAPTER FOUR

BREEDING METHODS

A great looking colt bred by Ball Quarter Horses, Fort Collins, Colorado.
(photo by Heidi Nyland)

HALLELUJAH!

Our treasured foundation mare, RDM Maar Hala, was twenty-three years old when we decided to breed her for one last time. She loved being a mother and was in great health. Maar Hala was also the Arabian breed's leading producer of Egyptian-bred champions. Because she'd been barren for four years, we brought her to a noted reproductive clinic. If anyone could help her conceive, they could.

At the same time, Maar Hala's champion son, El Halimaar, went briefly to the clinic to have his semen collected and frozen for shipment to a client's mare. Meanwhile, the clinic had successfully brought Maar Hala into heat. She was ovulating! But unfortunately, she didn't conceive with the shipped semen we'd ordered. We decided to have her stay with the veterinarians for another cycle, and pretty much gave them carte blanche with her.

But the next month we brought her home, without success, we thought. Maar Hala was in robust health and that was all that mattered.

The following March, the veterinarian visited the farm, and my father was with him as he examined Maar Hala. The vet looked at him seriously, and said, "Dr. Cruz, you'd better sit down."

"Maar Hala is pregnant." Well, *my father was thrilled!* Hallelujah! *When he calmed down, he asked the vet who was the father was.*

"Why, that magnificent stallion of yours—El Halimaar." With that, my father's mood changed considerably. He told the veterinarian that El Halimaar was the mare's son. Dad said he couldn't repeat what the vet replied! As you might imagine, there was some discussion of six-legged horses with three eyes and so on.

Well, we all took a deep breath and awaited the birth. After all (we told ourselves), some horse breeders use inbreeding to intensify the good characteristics of their breeding stock.

Later that summer, Maar Hala delivered a simply gorgeous filly. She was perfect in every way. And our cherished mare once more had a youngster to love and nurture. The filly would be her last.

And the filly's name? The word my father first spoke when he learned of the pregnancy, followed by her mother's initials: Haliluyah MH.

—*Dr. Jody Cruz, Rancho Bulakenyo, Los Osos, California*

You've decided to breed your special mare. She has a clean bill of health from your veterinarian, and is ready to breed. You've done your homework, and narrowed your stallion selection to four excellent candidates. One is local and available to be bred by live cover; two, both halfway across the country, are managed at stallion stations, and their cooled semen is shipped to mare owners; the fourth, a champion stallion and noted sire, now aged, has frozen semen available for purchase. What should you know about each of these breeding methods, and what are the pros and cons?

For answers, we went to Whit Byers, who has a master's degree in reproductive physiology from Colorado State University. With Paul Loomis (owner of Select Breeders Service Maryland), Byers owns Select Breeders Service Southwest, in Aubrey, Texas, with affiliate labs in California, Florida, and Italy. Byers's home is Siaset Farm in Aubrey, where he and his wife, Kathy, breed horses of their own. (Note that embryo transfer will be discussed in the following chapter.)

Your Timeline

First, you'll need your calendar when planning the breeding. The gestation period for horses may run from 315 to 365 days—or from 10½ to more than 12 months. If you live in California or Florida, your foal may scamper through fresh grass, enjoying 60-degree weather in January. No problem. However, if you reside in Michigan, you may want to schedule the birth for gentler months, when the snow has gone and warm sunshine will blanket your newborn.

You should also consider the usual temperature in your area at the time you intend to breed. "Owners should be aware that conception and fertility rates decline in extreme summer heat," Byers says. "In Texas, after a spell of 110-plus degree days, we always find that some mares' ovulation and some stallions' sperm production are negatively impacted." Worst case scenario: Heat can actually prevent conception.

Once you've decided when to breed your mare, you're ready to select the breeding method.

LIVE COVER

For centuries in the wild, stallions have bred their bands of mares without any intervention or assistance from man. As nature intended, this may be the ideal method for breeding horses. However, our domesticated horses are seldom "pasture bred." The most common exceptions are large ranches that turn a stallion out with their mares for the entire breeding season. And occasionally, owners try pasture breeding as a last resort for horses unable to otherwise breed successfully. Sometimes, with surprisingly good results.

Today, breeding by live cover usually refers to "hand breeding," where the stallion and mare are brought together by handlers for teasing and breeding.

"Live cover is not uncommon with very small breeding operations," Byers says. "The advantage is they don't have to gear up with equipment to collect and evaluate semen. And there's little or no additional overhead.

"The disadvantages include lack of ability to evaluate the stallion's semen, and chance of injury to the stallion and possibly the mare," he continues. "During hand breeding, the mare is generally restrained with a twitch, hobbles, and/or drugs. There's also an increased risk to the mare and stallion handlers. But where horses are routinely bred this way with experienced personnel, it's common to see a smooth operation using this method."

Teasing

Some mares, especially those being bred for the first time and those with foals, are difficult to recognize if they're in heat. A veterinarian will need to frequently palpate or use ultrasound on these mares to determine when they're ready to be bred. However, most mares, when introduced across a safe barrier (such as a solid fence) to a stallion, will show interest if they're in heat. This is called "teasing" and is used to determine whether a mare is ready to be bred. (See chapter 2.)

The teasing stallion may or may not be the breeding stallion. Sometimes, he's an aged stallion, or even a "stud-y" gelding. But the response is the same.

A mare in heat may nuzzle the stallion, and even turn her hind end to him. She will often lift her tail over her back, and spread her hind legs and squat. She may urinate, and afterward, open and close her vulva ("winking"). When she presents these signs, she's ready to be bred.

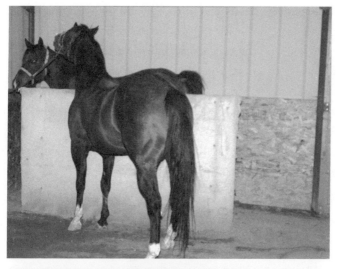

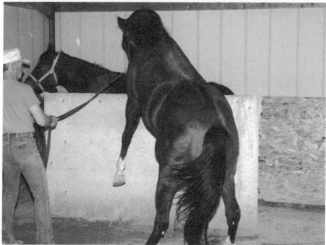

Quarter Horse World and All American Quarter Horse Congress champion TNT Fluid Fred is teased in the breeding barn at Ball Quarter Horses. (photos by Heidi Nyland)

Preparation

To prepare a mare for breeding, her tail should be wrapped from the top of the tail, down, for approximately twelve inches (use Vetrap, Elastikon, or special tail wraps, all readily available at equine-supply stores). Be careful not to cut off her circulation by wrapping too tightly.

The area under the mare's tail and around the vulva should be washed with a mild soap, rinsed with a mild solution of Betadine to disinfect it, and then gently but thoroughly rinsed again with warm, clean water. This is important to avert infection. The stallion's penis should be cleansed similarly. In both cases, the water rinse is vital to prevent irritation of sensitive areas, and to eliminate the disinfectant from entering the vagina and killing the sperm.

The breeding follows with the stallion mounting the mare. Every stallion handler has a routine that works best for a specific stallion. But always, it's vital that both horses are prepared and guided by experienced handlers, with safety a paramount consideration.

If you're planning to breed your mare by live cover, ask the stallion handler about his horse's manners and breeding style.

- How many mares does the stallion breed per season?
- What is his conception rate?

Particularly if you're planning to breed early in the year, be aware that if a stallion hasn't bred for six months or longer, it may take several breedings or semen collections (called *clean-out collections*) for him to produce quality semen.

It also can be very informative to speak with another mare owner about their experience breeding to that particular stallion—it should give you a good indication of what to expect.

ARTIFICIAL INSEMINATION

Artificial insemination (AI) is a breeding method in which semen collected from a stallion is placed in the mare. If the mare is on the premises, she may be bred immediately. Today, cooled semen is routinely shipped cross-country to mare owners and their veterinarians for insemination. Cooled semen is processed before transporting it to the mare owner for insemination—ideally within twenty-four to thirty-six hours after it's collected from the stallion. In recent years, semen that's been collected, processed, and frozen has increasingly come into use.

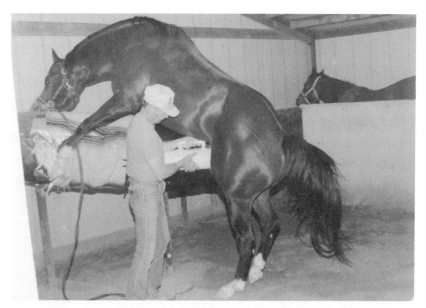

The stallion mounts a phantom or "dummy" mare for semen collection.
(photo by Heidi Nyland)

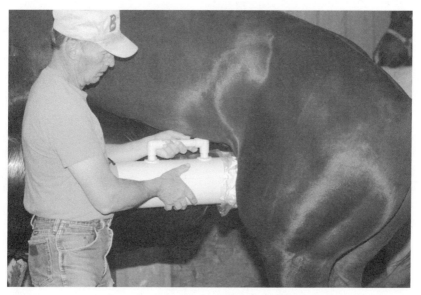

Collection, demonstrated by breeding manager Tom Ball, Ball Quarter Horses.
(photo by Heidi Nyland)

Read on, as Whit Byers answers some of the most commonly asked questions about AI, and the use of cooled shipped semen and frozen semen.

What are the pros and cons of using AI?

Artificial insemination has several advantages. An ejaculate can be collected and divided between several mares, thus utilizing the stallion's sperm production to its maximum potential. If semen is collected via mounting the stallion on a phantom mare—called a *dummy mare*—there's likely less danger to the stallion and to personnel. Semen collected for artificial insemination can be evaluated prior to insemination or cooling. The semen is evaluated for sperm count and percentage of *progressively motile* (relatively straight-moving) sperm. This assumes that the breeder or their veterinarian is equipped with a good microscope and sperm counter.

Artificial insemination does require cleanliness standards and knowledge of insemination techniques to be successful. *Semen extenders* (diluting substances) are commonly used in AI breeding. A stallion should be tested to see which semen extender will provide the best survival of the sperm and antibiotic protection.

What professional help should mare owners seek?

It's imperative that mare and stallion owners be trained by professionals in the field. Their experience level typically reflects the results they'll obtain. Their veterinarian is the first line of education. They may wish, as many do, to allow the veterinarian to do all the breeding work, including collection, processing, and insemination of the semen. Others hire breeding managers to do this work or work with the farm's veterinarian as a breeding team.

A solid AI program will require the veterinarian's expertise in palpating mares and using ultrasound scans. Timing of insemination is important especially when stallions are booked to large numbers of mares. Sperm production must be managed carefully during a long breeding season. Mares may need to be spaced throughout the season or skipped in order to have enough semen to achieve pregnancy. It's critical in a large breeding program to know the quality and amount of the stallion's semen you are dealing with. This will dictate how many mares may be bred. We find that semen quality varies greatly from horse to horse. If a stallion produces large numbers of sperm with acceptable *motility* (degree of movement), life is generally good. Stallions with large numbers of abnormal sperm or low sperm production can be a challenge.

Is all cooled shipped semen created equal?

No! As mentioned earlier, the quality of semen used for AI and cooled shipments are very stallion dependent. Some stallions do not cool well. Others do. That makes test cooling important. Although a stallion's semen cools well in one extender, it may cool even better in another one. If you don't try most of them, you won't know for sure. There are new extenders and protocols being developed all the time.

We and others offer a test-cooling service that helps stallion owners get their breeding program off on the right foot. Stallion owners should keep in mind that every mare they get in foal on the first cycle bred is one less to deal with later in the season. It's also one less unhappy mare owner.

After years and years of experience, I've observed that when mares don't get in foal with cooled semen, half the time it's because the mare or mare-management program is problematic. However, the other 50 percent that

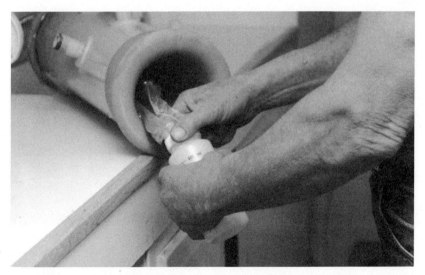

Emptied into a container, the semen is then mixed with an extender for shipment. (photo by Heidi Nyland)

57

don't get in foal is the result of poor-quality or badly handled semen from the stallion owner.

It's not wise to continually blame problems on "the other guy." You must know what you're doing. If you have a problem, call someone with lots of training, expertise, and experience to evaluate your management and handling protocols. Most of the time, the correction of small details adds up to big improvements.

What can a mare owner do to help ensure success?

The most important thing a mare owner can do is select a stallion that has proven fertility results, good semen quality, and lots of it. Of course, choosing

---

A COUNTRY DOC

Dr. Robert Mobray has been practicing veterinary medicine on Washington's Olympic Peninsula for nearly forty years. And almost every year, his satisfied clients vote the lifelong horseman with the irrepressible attitude, "the best" veterinarian in the area. While most of his clients utilize live cover breeding, he performs an average of twelve artificial inseminations per year with cooled shipped semen.

"There's an equation for successful AI: Start with a mare in good breeding health, add a fertile stallion, make sure both have conscientious owners—and you have a foal," he says smiling. "But remember, it only takes one weak link to prevent a pregnancy from occurring."

Fortunately, Dr. Mobray says, that's rare nowadays. "Our success rate is more than 90 percent. Everyone is more persistent—and consistent—than years ago."

Dr. Mobray *loves* the babies, and has bred a few notables of his own. His senior mare, Dolly Par Doc, a.k.a. "Phyllis," has produced six foals, including Docs Little Cowboy, a National Reining Horse Association champion. In her youth, his broodmare supreme also ran reining patterns, cut cattle, and packed Doc Mobray's eighty-four-year-old dad into the Olympic Mountains.

"You know, it sounds corny, but even after four decades, I'm still thrilled every time I deliver a foal," the good doctor says. "And first-time breeders will find it's even more special when that newborn is their own."

---

a highly fertile mare helps a great deal. Using a qualified reproductive veterinarian will also increase your chances of success.

Interestingly, on numerous occasions we've seen where the housing of the stallion can affect his semen quality. (This is now confirmed by university data.) Lights on stallions, used to maintain a short haircoat, will, over time, cause semen quality to deteriorate on some stallions. Also, housing a non-dominant stallion with other more dominant stallions can cause a decrease in his sperm numbers, as well as semen quality and libido.

So, if there are semen-quality issues, simple housing changes can often make a big difference.

What information about cooled shipped semen should mare owners obtain in preparation for breeding?

They need to know the motility before shipping, the anticipated motility after arrival, the number of sperm in a breeding dose and this stallion's success with cooled semen. The sperm's progressive motility at twenty-four hours should not be less than 50 percent initially, and shouldn't fall below 30 percent when cooled over a forty-eight hour period.

The correct dilution of semen is also important to success. It must be done accurately, using a minimum of one part semen to three parts extender. The final sperm concentration should be between twenty-five and fifty million per milliliter. The total number of progressively motile cells should be at least one billion. There are techniques—such as centrifugation and collecting a sperm-rich fraction—that can help some horses that have low concentrations of cells and poor motility to work adequately in a cooled semen program.

What time frame works for AI?

Ideally, a mare should be bred as close to ovulation as possible. Within twenty-four hours before to twelve hours after ovulation is okay if you're breeding to a highly fertile stallion. Poorer quality semen should be used as close to ovulation as possible.

Is cooled semen shipped with any information?

Many stallion managers send a collection form with cooled semen to assist the veterinary professional. It should include:

- The collection day and time.
- The volume of semen (both raw and diluted).
- The sperm count of the collection, and the total number of sperm (one billion progressively motile) in that specific shipment.
- The dilution ratio used when mixing the extender with the semen.
- The specific antibiotic and extender utilized.
- The end sperm concentration of the diluted semen.

Is frozen semen reliable? How is it stored?

The latest data indicates that on average and across stallions, properly produced frozen semen has very similar conception rates as cooled semen. Again, as with cooled semen, success is stallion dependent. Some stallions do as well with frozen semen as they do with cooled semen, or even on-farm breeding. And there are a few stallions that just do not work in a frozen program.

If stored properly, frozen stallion semen has an indefinite shelf life. It's stored in *cryo-containers* containing liquid nitrogen.

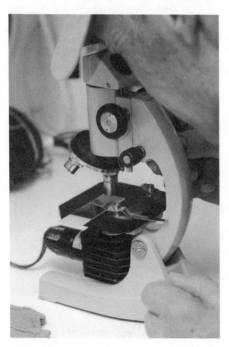

Microscopic scrutiny helps reveal semen quality. (photo by Heidi Nyland)

What questions should the mare owner ask the stallion manager about frozen semen?

Ask what the semen's post-thaw progressive motility is. The industry standard seems to be at least 30 percent progressive motility. As stated, there are a small number of stallions that simply don't do well in a frozen-semen program. They have sufficient motility with cooled semen, but low or nonexistent fertility with frozen semen. Conversely, a few stallions with motility of less than 30 percent will be found to do very well in a frozen-semen program.

Also ask what the stallion's conception rate is. If there's fertility information available, it'll help you determine how successful the stallion is in the frozen-semen program.

It's also important to know how many semen straws are in an insemination dose. This may vary from lab to lab, and can range from one to eight straws. Also the size of the straw (0.5ml or 5ml) will determine the temperatures for thawing. This is very important information. A thawing protocol should be sent with and/or ahead of the semen.

Does a reproductive specialist need special training to use frozen semen?

It's really quite simple to use. A good thermometer is about all the technical equipment you need. The 0.5ml straws must be thawed at body temperature (37 degrees Centigrade or 100 degrees Fahrenheit). The thaw time is about thirty seconds. The straws are then inseminated similarly to cooled semen in most cases. On the other hand, 5ml straws are thawed at about 45 to 50°C for forty-five seconds. This water is quite hot. So it's important to know what size the straws are, and to time the thawing accurately to prevent cooking the sperm.

(photo by Heidi Nyland)

Is frozen semen more expensive to use than cooled shipped semen?

It's best for mare owners to get a printed fee sheet from the stallion owner or manager, because there are many differences between stallion programs. It's interesting to note that a study done two to three years ago by Ed Squires, DVM, of Colorado State University at Fort Collins, showed that on average, frozen semen was a bit less expensive to use than cooled semen. Again, this will be stallion- and breeding-program dependent.

Whichever breeding method one uses, veterinarian fees for ultrasounds, palpation, and reproductive treatments need to be discussed with the practitioner before breeding season begins.

CHAPTER FIVE

EMBRYO TRANSFER

He'll steal your heart big time—a Miniature Horse foal bred by **Winsome, Etc. Miniatures, Monroe, Washington.** (photo by Jay Goss)

LIKE MOTHER, LIKE DAUGHTER?

Several years ago, we used embryo transfer in order to get a purebred Arabian foal from our Canadian champion futurity filly, Gai Acaisha. She was absolutely my favorite mare—you'd be hard-pressed to find another prettier or more charming. We bred her to our stallion, Saladins Allon, also a Canadian national champion. As you can imagine, my husband, Harold, and I were filled with excitement and anticipation about their offspring.

Our recipient mare, Fanny, was a wonderful "incubator" and flawless mother, but probably the most unattractive mare I'd ever seen. She had very short legs, and as Harold would say, a "big ol' jug head." She began showing signs of imminent birth about a month before her due date, so we took her to a renowned equine-reproductive center nearby, where they carefully managed her care for the next two weeks. Then, late one Friday night, we got the call that a perfect little filly had arrived without complication.

However, before sunrise the following morning we had another call—a frantic voice asked us to come to the clinic as soon as possible. When we arrived, a technician whom we hadn't previously met greeted us at the door. As we hurried to Fanny's stall, she muttered anxiously that she wasn't sure how "it" had happened.

Finally, the stall door opened to reveal our Fanny, proudly standing beside the tiniest, most exquisite Arabian filly we'd ever seen. Mother and daughter were the picture of peace and contentment. We turned to the young woman, still wringing her hands, shaking her head, and softly saying, "I just don't know how it happened."

Harold and I looked at each other—at once we knew what she'd presumed, and we burst out laughing. The poor girl, unfamiliar with dear Fanny, couldn't imagine that the petite Arabian filly could come from such a, well, "big" mare, and feared some grievous baby-swapping had transpired overnight! We explained the situation, and everyone sighed with relief.

A few weeks later, as Harold and I watched the filly, now named Gwenllian E, prance around her solicitous dam, he suggested we move them to our front pasture, so passersby could enjoy them, too. He also suggested posting a sign: "See how our stallion improved on this mare—imagine what he could do for yours!"

—Elizabeth Green, owner, Evergreen Arabians, Los Olivos, California

IT'S BEEN MORE THAN THIRTY YEARS SINCE THE FIRST EQUINE embryo transfer was performed in Japan. Today, the procedure has gained acceptance among breeders and breed organizations alike, because of its demonstrable benefits to mare owners, and its high rate of success when performed by an increasing number of knowledgeable equine practitioners.

Simplified, embryo transfer (ET) is the process of recovering an embryo from a bred mare (the donor) and transferring it to another mare (the recipient) that carries the foal to term.

We asked Robert Foss, DVM, of Equine Medical Services, Inc., in Columbia, Missouri, to explain about embryo transfer: the mares involved, the planning, the procedure, the success rate, and cost. EMS offers a wide array of farm, surgical, and outpatient services; in addition, it's a national leader in equine-assisted reproduction. At EMS, veterinarians perform approximately 400 embryo transfers annually. It also keeps a herd of 550 recipient mares available to their clients.

"Years ago, I'd never have predicted the remarkable advancements in the field," says Dr. Foss. "It's an amazing process, and for many mares and mare owners, it's provided foals otherwise unattainable."

THE PROCEDURE

Dr. Foss tells us that today, embryo-transfer technology is straightforward, and that the success rate has increased significantly with experience. Whether the embryo recovery and transfer takes place at the transfer facility or the embryo is shipped to the facility, the initial process is the same.

The sequence for embryo recovery goes like this:

1. The donor mare is bred and ovulates.

2. Seven to eight days following ovulation, a catheter is inserted into the mare's uterus, which is flushed with three to four separate liters of an electrolyte/nutrient solution.

3. The solution is then passed through a filter, which retains the embryo.

4. The embryo is recovered using a microscope. A seven-day-old embryo is about the size of a speck of dust, barely visible to the naked eye.

5. The embryo is evaluated, then given a grade from 1 to 5. Grade 1 embryos have no structural abnormalities; Grade 2 have minor abnormalities that aren't expected to interfere with a pregnancy; Grade 3 have more significant abnormalities that may reduce the chances of a successful transfer; Grade 4 have severe abnormalities that make pregnancy unlikely; Grade 5 are dead.

6. The viable embryo is washed to remove debris and contaminants, and placed into a nutrient medium.

7. The embryo is placed into a semen straw, then a transfer gun, which is inserted through the cervix of the recipient mare and into her uterus.

That transfer is the trickiest part of the entire procedure. "The embryo is a delicate little structure," Dr. Foss says. "It looks like a hollow balloon and is

(photo by Cappy Jackson)

easily damaged." Ideally, the recipient mare has ovulated two days after the donor mare, but the window of opportunity is actually one day before to three days afterward.

Following the transfer, the first pregnancy checks are on Day 5 and 7 following the transfer, which would be Days 12 and 14 after ovulation. After the confirmation of pregnancy at thirty days, the recipient mare may go home with the happy breeder.

DONOR-MARE CANDIDATES

Before you consider using your mare as an embryo-transfer donor candidate, check in advance with your breed registry for current registration guidelines and necessary paperwork for multiple foals from individual mares. Also—just as you would for any mare about to be bred—arrange for a breeding-soundness evaluation. (See chapter 2.) Embryo transfer allows you to overcome some challenges in these areas. (See chapter 6.)

Donor-mare candidates with reproductive challenges might include, for example:

Mares that foal late in the current season.

ET can ensure an early foal the next season, while leaving your mare open through the winter and available for early breeding that spring.

Mares with reproductive challenges.

These mares have conditions that either prevent or make it difficult for them to conceive, maintain a pregnancy, or safely give birth.

Young fillies.

ET enables breeding of young fillies whose bodies aren't yet mature enough to sustain a pregnancy.

Otherwise barren mares.

Even with ET, these candidates are more challenging, but they can achieve successful pregnancies.

(photo by Cappy Jackson)

ET also offers tremendous convenience. Donor-mare candidates in this category might include, for example:

Mares currently showing or in training.

The physical demands of certain show disciplines preclude pregnancy, and sometimes the stress of showing is such that mares don't produce well until they're out of training. ET allows these mares to continue their schedule almost uninterrupted, while at the same time producing sought-after foals.

Champion and champion-producing mares.

ET allows owners to obtain more than one foal per year from these valuable top producers.

RECIPIENT MARES

Recipient mares and recipient mare management is certainly a growth industry in the equine world. Today, most large embryo-transfer facilities provide these equine incubators for their clients. In large part, Dr. Foss says, this is because these mares are so important to the process.

"Embryo transfer is a game of minutiae, and even the smallest detail becomes vitally important to ensure success," he says. "One of the most detail-filled parts of the ET procedure is the transfer of the embryo from the donor to the recipient mare. The estrous cycles of both mares must be in sync, and our timing must be impeccable."

Additionally, since the recipient mare provides a healthful environment for the foal to grow, her constitution and reproductive tract must be robust. The veterinarians at EMS work hard to maintain a high-quality herd, which helps ensure the high rate of success their clients seek. They've also found that it's more expedient and effective to provide recipient mares for their clients, rather than having clients look for, evaluate, and prepare recipient mares themselves.

The ideal recipient mare, in addition to being sound and in excellent reproductive health, starts her career between the ages of four and ten years old. Robust, big-bodied (but not overweight) mares are desirable, and there are many breeds present in the EMS recipient herd.

Recently, the greatest challenge is finding enough recipient mares for the burgeoning ET business. Between 2003 and 2005, EMS professionals noted a 25 to 30 percent increase in demand for their equine surrogate mothers.

PREPARATION

If you decide to breed your mare by embryo transfer, you must next choose whether to bring her to a transfer facility for the entire breeding and transfer process, or to divide the process into segments, which would then be done at different locations.

For example, you may breed your mare at home or at a stallion station, then transport her to a transfer facility, which will transfer the embryo to a

SHOWING BENEFIT

Clint Fullerton, who owns and operates his Fullerton Training and Management, Inc., in Oak Grove, Missouri, has utilized equine embryo transfer for the past half-dozen years. In 2005, he bred for twenty embryo-transfer foals with the help of Robert Foss, DVM, and Equine Medical Services, Inc.

Fullerton's barn is home to Paint and Quarter Horse mares with multiple world halter championships. As a result, ET has become an invaluable tool for his horse management. Currently, both the American Paint Horse Association and the American Quarter Horse Association allow multiple foals registered annually from individual mares.

"I utilize embryo transfer for my young show mares whose careers I'd rather not interrupt for pregnancy, or those we want multiple foals from," Fullerton says. "I also use it with my older, famous mares. ET allows me to continue to obtain their offspring without subjecting them to the pain or risk that pregnancy has for senior mares."

Fullerton breeds the donor mares at his farm, then hauls them to the EMS facility for the embryo recovery and transfer procedure. "The trickiest part is timing the donor and recipient mares cycles to each other," he says. "And Dr. Rob Foss and his crew handle that perfectly."

Fullerton leases the recipient mare from the EMS herd. When his recipient mare is vet-checked in foal at thirty days, he brings her back to his farm. She stays there throughout her pregnancy, the birth of the foal, and until the foal is weaned. Then the mare returns to the EMS facility.

"The EMS reproductive herd is very high quality," Fullerton says. "ET may sound technical and complicated, but I can testify that for me, it's been a no-nonsense procedure and very easy to accomplish."

His advice to anyone considering ET? "Don't experiment—find a proven professional to work with. When you see your newborn foal running around a pasture in the spring, I can guarantee you, it's worth it!"

recipient mare. Or, you may have your bred-mare's embryo *flushed* (removed) at a separate facility, then shipped to a transfer facility for the transfer process. Either way, coordination and timing are crucial to the procedure's ultimate success.

Hide 'n' seek: a Paint Horse colt with his dam. (photo by Cappy Jackson)

Because meticulous preparation makes the ET procedure easier and increases the probability of success, Dr. Foss has compiled the following suggestions for a donor-mare owner. Use these guidelines if you plan to have your mare bred at a transfer facility, or if you plan to transport your mare to the transfer facility post-breeding.

- Contact your breed registry to make certain you're in compliance with its requirements for the eventual registry of the resulting foal. Some registries require a permit before the embryo is transferred, and rules can change.

- If the donor mare is to be bred at the facility, inform the stallion owner, and exchange contact numbers all around. Transfer-facility personnel will need to know the stallion's semen-collection schedule so they can order semen for your mare.
- Donor mares should have a Coggins test (for equine infectious anemia) performed in the current calendar year. All non-maiden mares should arrive with clean cultures.
- Donor-mare owners should provide written records of recent vaccinations and dewormings, so they aren't unnecessarily repeated. Include complete instructions for any special care that your mare requires.
- Donor mares that arrive for early breeding (before March 15) should be under lights at their home barn for at least eight weeks prior to the planned breeding.
- Coordination and communication regarding donor-mare arrival is imperative. Note that at EMS, there may be ninety to one hundred donor mares at any one time.

If you plan to have your bred-mare's embryo flushed at a separate facility, then shipped to a transfer facility, Dr. Foss has another set of procedural suggestions:

- Contact your breed registry.
- Communicate with your veterinarian to make certain he or she is prepared.
- Contact the transfer facility when your donor mare ovulates. This information allows the facility time to select and prepare a recipient mare whose estrous cycle coincides with your mare. Failure to do this in a timely manner will undermine the success of the procedure.
- Determine whether your veterinarian has the special shipping media necessary for the embryo. If not, the transfer facility can usually provide it.
- Make shipping and courier arrangements early to avoid last-minute disappointment.

- Always notify the transfer facility when the embryo flush is completed, regardless of the outcome. If an embryo has been recovered, the facility will prepare for its arrival; if not, facility personnel should be aware that they don't need to look for your shipment, and they'll manage the recipient mare accordingly.
- And finally, after the recipient mare is vet-checked in foal at thirty days, give at least seventy-two hours' notice before picking her up. Mares are often kept at satellite farms, so will need to be brought back to the facility.

(photo by Cappy Jackson)

SUCCESS RATE & COST

Two separate steps in the embryo-transfer procedure have their own separate success rates. First is the embryo-recovery rate from the donor mare. Second is the verification of pregnancy in the recipient mare.

Embryo-recovery rates depend in large part on the fertility of the donor mare. Young, healthy mares have very high rates. As a rule, practitioners find that these mares produce a viable embryo 80 percent of the time, per cycle. In general, older mares with infertility issues have recovery rates of approximately 30 percent per cycle. Of course, there are always individuals whose recovery rates post higher or lower.

Once they've been recovered, Grades 1 and 2 embryos (perfect and very good, respectively) have a pregnancy success rate of approximately 80 percent. Grade 3 embryos are used less frequently. Why? Transfer success for Grade 3 embryos is typically in the 50 to 60 percent range. However, if your mare is otherwise barren, this might represent your only chance for a foal. Pregnancy rates for embryos recovered elsewhere and transported to the facility are approximately 5 percent lower than those recovered onsite.

The cost of embryo transfer varies between facilities, but to give you a general idea of what to expect, here's an average of prevailing costs nationwide.

A standard ET program-enrollment fee is approximately $1,400. This fee is usually nontransferable and nonrefundable. It covers the donor mare's ultrasound scan, artificial insemination, and embryo recovery and transfer. It also covers management of the donor mare through four estrous cycles; additional cycles are billed at $200 to $300 each. The enrollment fee also includes the preparation of the recipient mare for the transfer and the transfer itself.

When the recipient mare achieves thirty days gestation with a viable pregnancy, you'll lease her from the transfer facility for approximately $2,500, pick her up, and keep her at your own barn or boarding facility. (You'll probably return the recipient mare within six months of foaling, depending on the facility's policy.) After the pregnancy is thirty days old, you can hope for a live-foal guarantee. This guarantee will probably include a credit toward future ET procedures if the recipient mare doesn't produce a live foal. The transfer facility of your choice should have all the details spelled out in writing for you.

The boarding fee for both donor and recipient mares will vary, depending on accommodation (pasture, stall, or a combination of both); the fee ranges from $9 to $15 per day. Secure these arrangements in advance. Mare and foal board will run about $16 per day.

Keep in mind that the stallion's stud fee, semen shipping costs, and registration fees are separate—and also your responsibility.

Like the popular television commercial that tallies up the cost of goods and services, one can tally up embryo-recovery fees, transportation costs, and per diem board. But watching your newborn foal frisk and frolic across fresh spring grass? *Priceless!*

A high-stepping Morgan colt bred by Fire Run Farm. (photo by Jay Goss)

McQuay Stables Inc.
Embryo Transfer Contract

THIS CONTRACT and agreement is entered into on the date shown below, by and between McQuay Stables Inc. (hereinafter, "MS") and _____ , the Owner/ Lessee (hereinafter, "Owner/Lessee") of _____ , (horse's name) (hereinafter, "Donor Mare"). Owner/Lessee desires MS to perform an embryo transfer from Donor Mare to a suitable recipient, and MS agrees to perform such embryo transfer, upon the terms and conditions and for the consideration set forth herein.

1) This service is for the 20__ breeding season, commencing February 1 and closing July 15.

2) MS agrees to provide all reasonably necessary veterinary services to perform the transfer of one embryo from the Donor Mare to a Recipient Mare.

3) MS will exercise the ordinary standard of care in performing the transfer and caring for the Donor Mare that is generally accepted in the industry.

4) As consideration for the services to be performed by MS, Owner/ Lessee shall pay MS the sum of $2,500.00 for Recipient Mare and all veterinarian expenses shall be paid to Equine Medical Associates Inc. ($500.00 per flush, $250.00 per transfer)

   a) $2,500.00 is due and payable when the Recipient Mare checks thirty (30) days safe in foal.

   b) This contract grants one year right of return service in the event the Recipient Mare does not carry her pregnancy to term. This right of return service is in the event the Recipient Mare does not carry her pregnancy to term. This right comes in the form of a $2,500.00 credit on account toward one future embryo transfer to be used in the same or subsequent year's breeding season. The following provisions apply:

      i. A discontinuation of Progesterone and/or Estrogen Supplements given to Recipient Mare must be approved by MS or this contract becomes null and void with no right of return;

      ii. When the Recipient Mare is removed from MS, the Donor Mare Owner/Lessee agrees to provide a written veterinary certification that a live foal (standing and nursing) was not obtained;

      iii. If the Recipient Mare's failure to carry to term was due to an Act of God, or subquality care, management practices and/or negligence on the part of Owner/Lessee (or Owner/Lessee's agents), at MS's sole discretion, this right of return service provision becomes null and void;

      iv. MS reserves the right, at its sole discretion, to stipulate how said credit is to be applied, including any decision to transfer the credit to another Donor Mare or to refund the credit to Owner/Lessee; and

      v. The Recipient Mare is to be returned in healthy condition.

   c) In the event multiple embryos are recovered in a single flush, MS reserves the right to transfer all embryos. The Owner/ Lessee shall have the option to accept or reject the second transfer at the time both Recipient Mares are determined to be fourteen (14) days safe in foal. If both mares remain safe in foal at thirty (30) days, an additional fee of $2,500.00 shall be due and payable for the Recipient Mare. If Owner/Lessee rejects the second transfer or fails to pay all amounts due and owing to MS when due, Owner/Lessee's waives any and all claim(s) or right(s) to the second foal.

5) Owner/Lessee shall be responsible for all vet fees on the Recipient Mare after transfer. In the possible event an embryo is left in the Donor Mare's uterus, whether an embryo is recovered or not, it is the Owner/Lessee's responsibility to have the Donor Mare ultrasounded at 16–20 days post ovulation to ensure against an unwanted pregnancy. It is the Owner/Lessee's responsibility to terminate an unwanted pregnancy.

6) THE RECIPIENT MARE WILL BE RELEASED TO OWNER/LESSEE ON THE THIRTY-FIFTH DAY OF PREGNANCY, AT WHICH TIME ALL UNPAID FEES AND EXPENSES SHALL BE PAID IN FULL. Owner/Lessee agrees to pay MS the sum of $12.00 per day for pasture board of the Recipient Mare for each and every day the Recipient Mare remains after the thirty-fifth day of pregnancy. MS accepts VISA, MASTER-CARD, DISCOVER, and AMERICAN EXPRESS.

7) Owner/Lessee agrees that MS makes no guarantees as to the success of the transfer of quality or confirmation of the resulting foal, or that the resulting foal will be free of any infirmity, defect, disease, or inherited trait.

8) It is understood and agreed that MS, its agents, employees and assigns shall not be liable for any disease, accident, or disability of the Owner/Lessee, any person, personal property, Donor Mare, Recipient Mare, or resulting foal, and Owner/Lessee holds each of them harmless from any liability for same. Any insurance desired on the Donor Mare, Recipient Mare, and foal shall be at the sole expense and discretion of Owner/Lessee.

9) Owner/Lessee shall be responsible for complying with the applicable breed registry's rules and regulations for registration of the foal by embryo transfer. MS will maintain the records of identification on both the Donor and Recipient Mares to facilitate registration of the resulting foal by Owner/Lessee. Owner/Lessee shall provide MS with a copy of the Donor Mare's current registration at the time of signing this contract.

10) MS reserves the right to refuse to perform a transfer based solely upon the professional judgment of the attending veterinarian, including the right to discontinue transfer attempts or refuse to transfer any unsuitable embryo.

11) The lease of the Recipient Mare shall terminate upon the resulting foal being weaned, or upon the expiration of one year to date of impregnation, whichever occurs last. Upon termination, Lessee shall return Recipient Mare to MS in Tioga, Texas, in sound health, with a negative Coggins.

12) The Recipient Mare is the property of MS and is not for sale. Recipient Mare is to be returned to MS in good health. In the event the Recipient Mare is not returned due to selling embryo, disability, or death, Owner/Lessee agrees to provide a veterinarian's report and immediately tender $1,500.00 to MS.

13) A vaccination, worming, and farrier record will be sent with the Recipient Mare upon her departure from MS. Owner/Lessee shall be responsible for maintaining all normal and customary veterinary and farrier procedures to ensure the proper care and good health of Recipient Mare and foal.

14) Lessee will be responsible for all expenses of Recipient Mare in connection with normal and customary upkeep and maintenance during the time the Recipient is in Owner/Lessee's possession and care, and as further provided herein.

15) MS makes no representations, covenants or warranties, express or implied, with respect to the condition, merchantability, quality, suitability or fitness for any particular purpose of the Recipient Mare (**except that MS warrants that it or its officers has title to the Recipient Mare.**) With respect to Recipient Mare "as is" and "with all faults." MS is not liable for any damages caused by the Owner/Lessee. Owner/Lessee agrees that the Recipient Mare will not be ridden, driven, or used for any purpose other than to carry the in utero foal to term.

16) The obligations and undertakings of each of the parties to this Contract shall be performable in Grayson County, Texas, and shall be governed by and construed in accordance with the laws of the State of Texas. The parties agree that the proper venue for litigating any claims arising out of or incidental to this Contract shall be in Grayson County, Texas. Owner/Lessee agrees to pay all reasonable attorneys' fees incurred by MS in attempting to collect any outstanding balance due from Owner/Lessee.

17) This contract shall be binding upon and inure to the benefit of the heirs, successors, and assigns of the respective parties hereto.

18) WARNING: UNDER TEXAS LAW (CHAPTER 87, CIVIL PRACTICE AND REMEDIES CODE), AN EQUINE PROFESSIONAL IS NOT LIABLE FOR AN INJURY TO OR THE DEATH OF A PARTICIPANT IN EQUINE ACTIVITIES RESULTING FROM THE INHERENT RISKS OF EQUINE ACTIVITIES.

19) This contract contains the entire agreement between the parties with respect to the subject matter herein. Any oral representations or modifications concerning this Contract shall be of no force or effect unless contained in a subsequent writing, signed by the parties to be charged. Time is of the essence of this Contract.

EXECUTED AND AGREED the dates of our respective signatures below.

_____   _____

McQuay Stables Inc.   Date

BY: _____

_____   _____

Owner/Lessee   Date

PRINTED NAME: _____

ADDRESS: _____

HOME & BUSINESS PHONE: _____

MARE: _____ AGE: _____ BREED _____

REGISTRATION NUMBER: _____

MARE OWNER (IF LEASED): _____
***must provide MS with copy of Lease

STALLION: _____

RANCH CONTACT/PHONE: _____

FOR OFFICE USE: ( ) $1,000.00 booking fee ( ) Registration papers ( ) Coggins

_____   _____

Check #   Date Paid

CHAPTER SIX

BREEDING
THE PROBLEM MARE

A charming mare with her foal at Crown Morgans. (photo by Jay Goss)

HAPPY ACCIDENT

As a breeder of registered Morgan horses for more than twenty years I've witnessed many joyful, wondrous, and tragic situations in the breeding and foaling shed. One particularly interesting situation concerns a Morgan mare I purchased as a five-year-old. JMF After Eight ("Mahogany") was the epitome of everything I'd hoped and dreamed of producing. I could hardly wait to begin breeding this mare to my stallion of similar quality.

I purchased Mahogany in late fall. Early the following spring, I began teasing her with the stallion. Mahogany didn't respond in any of the usual ways and showed no signs of heat.

After several months, I had an ultrasound scan performed of Mahogany's uterus and ovaries. Everything checked out as normal. My veterinarian and I decided to put my mare on hormone therapy, so we could be sure of when ovulation would occur. Subsequent ultrasound scans revealed that Mahogany didn't ovulate when expected. There wasn't a sign of a single follicle.

I tried breeding Mahogany again over the course of several years. Each time, there were no follicles, and she continued to be totally disinterested in the stallion. Sadly, I accepted the fact that my lovely mare was sterile.

One summer, one of our weanlings needed equine companionship; I decided to try bonding the colt to Mahogany. The two quickly became inseparable.

But the following winter, I discovered the eleven-month-old colt mounting and breeding my "sterile" mare! I thought about separating them, because the colt was so young, but figured any "damage" was already done. Also, the colt's manners and breeding were impeccable.

The next summer, we saw the breeding behavior occur once more. I decided to have an ultrasound scan performed on Mahogany. Lo and behold, we had an embryo! Mahogany foaled a lovely black filly the following spring. She was an excellent mother, and everything proceeded normally.

Now we're trying again to breed Mahogany to my star stallion. With luck, I'll have my dream foal.

—Julie Bair,
Maritime Morgans, Waterford, Pennsylvania

STORIES LIKE THE ONE JULIE BAIR RELATES ABOUT HER MORGAN mare, Mahogany, abound in the equine world. Mares that have every reason to be fertile don't conceive. And "sterile" mares suddenly become pregnant, pleasantly surprising their owners.

If a mare is young, healthy, and fertile, chances are that she'll become pregnant easily and deliver a healthy foal, assuming she's well-managed and bred to a fertile stallion at the right time.

But some mares prove to be challenging, frustrating, and expensive to successfully breed—for a variety of reasons. Overcoming the obstacles associated with breeding a problem mare requires patience, vigilance, a competent veterinarian, and careful management.

If your mare doesn't conceive when you expect her to, don't despair. Here, equine-reproductive expert Jill (Thayer) Cook, DVM, lends her expertise and insight. First, she defines what's meant by a "problem mare." Then she discusses ten common breeding challenges, explaining where the problem lies, and what you can do to manage each one to enhance your mare's chance of conception, maintaining pregnancy, and delivering a healthy foal.

WHAT *IS* A PROBLEM MARE?

Veterinarians often define a problem mare as one that's failed to conceive over the duration of three cycles, assuming that there was good pre-breeding management and that the mare has been bred to a fertile stallion.

The problem mare faces two distinct issues. The first is getting into foal. Obviously, she can't produce a healthy foal if she never becomes pregnant. Second, she must maintain the pregnancy through the entire gestation period, an average of 340 days. Your problem mare might successfully achieve the first goal, but not the second.

A broodmare isn't always selected for her ability to reproduce. In fact, many mares are bred regardless of their reproductive health. You might select a broodmare because of her stellar pedigree, her successful performance record, and/or your emotional ties to her, all of which create a desire for a foal out of *that mare in particular.*

Snuggling with mom. (photo by Cappy Jackson)

While there's nothing wrong with these reasons to breed your mare, you also need to factor in her ability to conceive, maintain a pregnancy, and deliver a healthy foal. Something else to keep in mind: Fertility is a *heritable trait*, which means your problem mare's offspring might encounter similar or greater reproductive problems.

Technological advances, such as artificial insemination, embryo transfer, and advanced fertility treatments increase the possibility that your mare can overcome a number of breeding challenges. However, keep in mind that she will likely have an increased risk of complications related to pregnancy and delivery. And the extra effort and expense you'll put into breeding her may be significant.

Finally, be aware that there might come a time when, despite your best efforts, you'll need to consider giving up on breeding your problem mare, and move on to a more suitable broodmare candidate.

On the other hand, your problem mare might just need a little help from you and a knowledgeable veterinarian. Let's take a look at a few of the problems found most commonly in equine breeding, and what you and your vet can do about it.

COMMON BREEDING CHALLENGES

The following breeding challenges might make breeding your mare more difficult than if she was reproductively sound. (Note that weight-related challenges were discussed in chapter 3.)

Breeding challenge #1: Too young.

Why it's a problem: A mare less than two years old generally hasn't yet reached sexual maturity and simply can't be bred. Even if a two-year-old mare has reached puberty and appears to be cycling normally, she can be difficult to successfully breed at that age.

What you can do: Be patient! Wait to breed a young mare until she's reached full sexual maturity, which generally occurs at three years old. Some breeds mature more quickly, and your mare might be ready for conception as soon as she reaches age two, but it's best not to breed her until she's chronologically twenty-four months old. For example, if she was foaled in April, wait until the April of her two-year-old year to breed her. Consider breeding a young mare only if she's physically mature for her age, and do so only on the advice of your veterinarian.

Breeding challenge #2: Too old.

Why it's a problem: An older mare generally falls into one of two categories. The first includes a mare nine to twelve years old that might be a challenge to breed, but she doesn't yet fall into the problematic category. The degree to which she'll be a reproductive challenge may depend on the number of pregnancies she's carried. For example, if she's carried a number of foals, she might've developed cervical tearing, which we'll discuss in a bit.

The second category includes a mare more than sixteen years old whose fertility has simply declined due to the aging process. An older mare often has uterine infections and scarring throughout her reproductive system that can inhibit conception. (For details, see breeding challenges #5 and #6.) Also, her eggs might be genetically inferior, which leads to a high pregnancy-loss rate whether the embryo is carried by her or a recipient mare via embryo

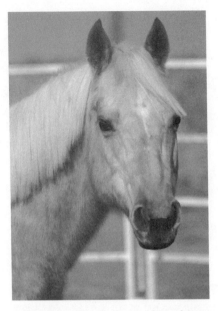

A fine example of an aged broodmare at Swalde Quarter Horses, Longmont, Colorado. (photo by Heidi Nyland)

transfer. She might also have age-related thinning and weakening. (For details, see breeding challenge #4). **What you can do:** With the help of your veterinarian, first try to determine the exact nature of your older mare's problem. Your older mare could be facing one or more of the breeding challenges discussed here, all of which must be carefully and completely handled before she can conceive and carry a foal.

Breeding challenge #3: Reproductive conformation.

Why it's a problem: A mare with potential reproductive problems might have excess slope to her vulva, or her vulvar lips might not seal completely. Further, a low pelvic bone or pulled-forward rectum can be problematic. Such conformation allows contaminants to invade her reproductive tract, causing irritation and infection, which can lead to infertility. Some contaminants are introduced via wayward fecal matter and *urine pooling*. That is, instead of urine evacuating completely outside the body, it splashes and pools in front of the cervix, which causes cervical irritation and can cause uterine infection.

Urine in the uterus also hinders conception and pregnancy, because neither sperm cells nor embryo can thrive in such a contaminated environment. Irritation can also prevent the embryo from attaching to the uterine wall and receiving nourishment.

Mares can inherit poor external reproductive conformation, or the problem might be associated with their breed characteristics. Age and repeated foaling also affect external conformation.

What you can do: Ask your veterinarian whether your mare would be a good candidate for Caslick's surgery. (See "What is Caslick's Surgery?") This procedure will form a protective barrier between exterior contaminants and

---

WHAT IS CASLICK'S SURGERY?

Dr. E. A. Caslick was a resident veterinarian at Claiborne, a prestigious Thoroughbred farm. Working to help mares conceive, he developed a procedure to correct ill-formed vulvas. He found that many mares couldn't remain pregnant, because debris and bacteria was vacuumed into the uterus due to poor vulvar conformation.

To fix the problem, Dr. Caslick removed a strip of tissue alongside a mare's vulva. Then he pressed the exposed tissue together and stitched partway down, from top to bottom. The vulva grafted together around the stitches. Mares that were once problem-breeders often conceive easily after Caslick's surgery.

The stitches must be removed prior to foaling and replaced soon after birth. If a mare foals with the Caslick's intact, she'll tear and need reconstructive work.

When you purchase a mare you think you might breed someday, find out whether she's had the surgery, so you can plan accordingly.

—*Heidi Immegart, DVM, MS, PhD*

---

the sensitive interior of your mare's reproductive system.

Breeding challenge #4: Age-related muscular thinning and weakening.

Why it's a problem: As a broodmare ages and carries numerous pregnancies, her entire reproductive tract tends to drop in her abdomen. Her abdominal muscles also lose tone, which can cause her vagina to slope downward near the urethral opening causing urine pooling. (For details, see breeding challenge #3.)

Your older mare might only experience urine pooling while

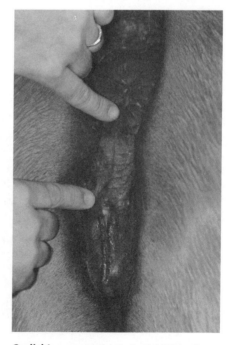

Caslick's surgery. (photo by Heidi Nyland)

she's in heat, when her muscles are relaxed. If so, then the problem will go away once her heat cycle completes and her muscles tighten. Or your mare might experience this problem all the time, which is more serious.

What you can do: If your mare experiences urine pooling solely due to weakened muscles during her heat cycle, your veterinarian can manage the problem by flushing out your mare's uterus when you're ready to breed. (Regular ultrasound scans can determine whether fluid within the uterus needs to be flushed.) If urine pooling is an ongoing issue, your mare might require a *urethral extension surgery*, which essentially extends her *urethra* (the tube that carries the urine out of the body) so she can fully evacuate urine away from her vagina.

Breeding challenge #5: Uterine infection.

Why it's a problem: Uterine infection can cause severe scarring, especially if the infection is prolonged or improperly treated. Infection also kills sperm. As mentioned earlier, uterine infection can result from reproductive conformation, which can allow bacteria, urine, and debris into the uterus. Breeding via live cover can also introduce contaminants into your mare's reproductive tract.

Note that unlike other animals, mares generally don't become noticeably ill when suffering from a uterine infection. However, an infected mare might have vaginal discharge and frequently has fluid in her uterus, which can be detected with an ultrasound scan.

What you can do: Talk to your veterinarian. He or she can take a uterine culture to find exactly what's going on. The swab is cultured for bacterial growth and sensitivity to antibiotics, which give your veterinarian information about how to treat the infection.

An *endometrial biopsy* can also offer valuable information. In this procedure, a small piece of your mare's uterine tissue is preserved and cross-sectioned so your veterinarian can evaluate its layers. The tissue is generally graded 1 through 3, with A and B subcategories; this grade reflects the likelihood that your mare will conceive and carry a foal to term.

The following list briefly describes each grade. All uterine infections require prompt attention to maintain your mare's reproductive future and general health.

1A: Completely normal.

1B: Minimal changes.

2A: Treatable changes requiring treatment.

2B: Major changes requiring aggressive treatment.

3A: Vast uterine scarring, indicating a poor prognosis for carrying a foal to term.

3B: Extensive scarring, necessitating a negative pregnancy prognosis.

Breeding challenge #6: Reproductive scarring.

Why it's a problem: Over time, pregnancy and foaling problems can scar and tear a mare's reproductive system, especially if she's had a number of foals. Extensive scarring can inhibit her ability to close her *cervix* (the outer end of the uterus), exposing her to infection. Scarring can be so severe that it completely closes the cervix, making the breeding process very difficult—a mare needs an open cervix for breeding.

Infection can cause scarring within the *oviduct* (also called the *fallopian tubes*, the egg's passageway). Oviduct scarring can hinder fertilization, because that's where the egg and sperm meet and merge.

(photo by Cappy Jackson)

SUCCESS STORY

A sixteen-year-old maiden mare had been successfully shown lo-
cally, until mild lameness ended her competitive career. She was cycling normally when her owners brought her to Dr. Jill (Thayer)
Cook at Royal Vista Equine one April for a breeding-soundness
evaluation.

The evaluation revealed that the mare's uterus contained fluid
with some particulate matter. A uterine culture showed heavy bacterial growth. An endometrial biopsy revealed the mare was suffering from a Grade 2A infection with inflammation. Further, the mare
was scheduled to be bred to a subfertile stallion via shipped semen.

Dr. Cook explained to the owner that breeding the mare would
be a challenge. At the time of the evaluation, the mare was in heat;
treatment began immediately to combat the infection. Dr. Cook
flushed the mare's uterus with saline and mild Betadine. She also
gave the mare *oxytocin* (a breeding hormone that causes uterine
contractions) and antibiotics for seven days.

During the mare's following heat cycle, Dr. Cook tested the
mare's uterine fluid again, and it appeared to be more normal. Dr.
Cook gave the mare another round of antibiotics. The mare was
then bred, but didn't conceive. However, the mare was successfully
bred during her next heat, and produced a healthy foal.

What you can do: Follow the advice of your veterinarian. Some cervical scarring responds to medical treatment or can even be reduced with surgery.
Oviduct scarring is difficult—and sometimes impossible—to correct.

Breeding challenge #7: Cervix fails to open.

Why it's a problem: Again, a mare needs an open cervix for breeding. Also, if
the cervix doesn't open, she'll retain uterine fluid that she'd otherwise evacuate to maintain reproductive health. In addition to cervical scarring, outlined
earlier, hormonal problems can hinder a mare's ability to open her cervix.

What you can do: To manage cervical scarring, see the previous breeding
challenge. If your mare has hormonal problems that affect her ability to open
her cervix, consider artificial insemination, which introduces sperm directly
into your mare's uterus.

To evacuate retained uterine fluid, your veterinarian will flush your mare's uterus with a large volume of fluid (called *lavage*). Your vet might also give your mare supplemental *estrogen* (a reproductive hormone) to balance her hormone levels. Note that a mare's cervix will often return to normal once she carries a foal to full-term.

Breeding challenge #8: Uterine cysts.

Why they're a problem: Actually, small uterine cysts usually don't cause reproductive problems. In fact, cysts are common in older mares that have foaled multiple times. Cysts sit on pedestals—they're not wide-based—and are a lot like fluid-filled blisters.

Large cysts or a high number of cysts can interfere with pregnancy. Although cysts are inactive, they do occupy space along the uterine lining, which can reduce an embryo's ability to extract nutrition. Cysts can even cause late-term abortion. And there's another problem with cysts: If a tiny, traveling embryo lodges next to one, it can be difficult for an ultrasound

(photo by Cappy Jackson)

(photo by Cappy Jackson)

scan to determine whether a mare is pregnant. Likewise, a cyst might be mistaken for an embryo. (Tip: Have your mare scanned before she's bred, so you and your veterinarian will know where your mare's cysts are located.)

What you can do: Follow the advice of your veterinarian. If your mare's cysts are smaller than a dime, your vet will typically recommend that they be left alone, as aggressive treatment can prove detrimental to your mare's reproductive health. However, if cysts are interfering with the pregnancy, laser removal is often successful.

Breeding challenge #9: Abnormal cycles.

Why it's a problem: During a mare's transitional period at the beginning and end of the breeding season, she'll most likely have abnormal cycles. Obese mares are particularly prone to abnormal cycles. During an abnormal cycle, a mare might show signs of heat for seven to sixty days without building a large follicle. Or, she might produce an *anovulatory follicle*. This follicle usually isn't fertile and can delay a mare's heat cycle.

What you can do: Schedule ultrasound scans to see exactly what's going on in your mare's reproductive tract, then follow the advice of your veterinarian.

Breeding challenge #10: The stallion's fertility.

Why it's a problem: Of course, it takes both mare and stallion to make a foal. If you can't find anything wrong with your mare—or you've been able to fully manage her breeding challenges—and she still fails to conceive, it might be time to consider the stallion as the problem.

What you can do: Have an open, non-offensive conversation with the stallion's owner or manager, preferably before attempting to breed your mare to the stallion. Ask about the stallion's fertility evaluation and the number of mares he successfully bred the previous year.

If you plan to breed your mare with shipped semen, ask about the veterinary practices used to prepare the ejaculate. Is a sperm count taken before the ejaculate ships? Are the sperm *motile* (active) and healthy? Does his semen cool/freeze and ship well?

If possible, speak with others who've bred their mares to the stallion. Ask about the successes they achieved or obstacles they faced. Get as much information as possible to ensure you breed your mare to a fertile stallion. (See chapter 4.)

(photo by Cappy Jackson)

CHAPTER SEVEN

STALLION SELECTION

A kind and elegant stallion, Ali Saroukh, of Silver Maple Farm.
(photo by Darryl Larson)

HITTING THE JACKPOT

In 1982, my husband, Phil, and I bought the farm of our dreams in Ashland, Ohio. Two years later, I went to a spring horse sale, looking for a two-year-old Quarter Horse prospect to show, then sell. I'd convinced Phil that this strategy would help my horse habit pay for itself.

Well, I drove home with a sixteen-year-old broodmare in my trailer, heavy in foal to a stallion named Zippo Pine Bar. The stallion had been the 1972 American Quarter Horse Association national high-point junior Western pleasure horse and Western riding stallion. But his offspring were still largely an unknown quantity.

What would my husband think? Fortunately, as always, he supported me completely.

When my mare, Fancy Blue Chip, foaled, the colt was outstanding, so I put Fancy back into the trailer and drove her to Nebraska to be bred back to Zippo Pine Bar. My goal was to breed Western pleasure horses. Fancy didn't have a show record, but she had a crisp, flat jog, and a correct, cadenced lope. And Zippo Pine Bar was a slow, fluid mover, with long strides. They were a wonderful nick.

When their second foal hit the ground I knew I'd hit the jackpot! Zips Chocolate Chip had the same, soft way of moving as a youngster that he has today. He just never had an awkward stage.

After a successful show career that included the unanimous 1989 AQHA world junior Western pleasure championship, Zips Chocolate Chip began his breeding career. He became the first double inductee into the National Snaffle Bit Association Hall of Fame, based on both his show and sire records, and is an all-time leading AQHA Western pleasure sire.

Just think, when I hauled Fancy back to Nebraska and her date with Zippo Pine Bar, the breeding fee was $700, and mare care was $3 per day. That was certainly the best investment I've ever made!

—Ann Myers, Myers Horse Farms, Ashland, Ohio

ANN MYERS'S STORY ILLUSTRATES HOW BOTH SERENDIPITY AND planning influence stallion selection. She purchased Fancy Blue Chip because the mare possessed correct conformation and gaits suitable for producing Western pleasure horses, which was Myers's breeding goal. *Great strategy.* Fancy was already in foal to a stallion who a dozen years earlier had been the AQHA national high-point junior Western pleasure horse. *Good fortune, and another step in the right direction.* Then, when the first colt was good, Myers bred again, and the second colt was great. *She hit the jackpot!*

But, whoa! You say, if selecting the right stallion for a mare was that straightforward, everyone would do it with spectacular results—and you're right. There are a multitude of variables unique to every breeding—and each time is a roll of the dice.

For the record, Ann Myers looks at every breeding as "a surprise package." She bred Fancy Blue Chip to Zippo Pine Bar seven times, successfully every time, but in varying degrees. Just as there are only so many super novas in the firmament, equine superstars are a rarity.

Breeding horses is always a bit of a gamble. But while there are no guarantees, if you do your homework and attend to details, you can make decisions that will stack the odds in your favor.

We asked experienced horse breeders what their considerations are when selecting a stallion. They consider the stallion's conformation and prepotency—that is, his tendency to pass on his strengths to his offspring. They also note the disposition, pedigree, and the show and breeding records when selecting a stallion. Breeders ask themselves, "Will this stallion's strengths in these areas complement my mare?"

Mare owners should make certain the stallion is managed so that breeding is conducted in a professional, timely manner that reliably results in client success. If breeders plan to sell the foal, they should take note of any marketing program for offspring the stallion owner might offer, through their Web site or annual production sales. If breeders intend to show the foal, if one stallion under consideration offers an incentive fund for offspring that become show champions, that might be a deal maker.

As you'll see, the amount of emphasis placed on each element varies dramatically from one breeder to another, which proves one thing: There are many pathways to the ultimate goal—a successful breeding.

CONFORMATION

George Zbyszewski of George Z Training in Auburn, Washington, manages the Arabian stallion, *Emanor, for owners Ron and Mila Hart of Windhorse Farm in Santa Ynez, California. *Emanor, a national champion in his native Poland, is also a U.S. Arabian national champion stallion and Canadian national champion park horse, one of the most demanding of the English disciplines.

George Z advises numerous mare owners on their stallion selection, and rates conformation as his primary consideration. "First, I believe a professional evaluation of the mare and her conformation is an excellent investment, because 'barn blindness' can lead to expensive breeding mistakes," he says. "Mare owners can be very emotionally involved with their horse—not a bad thing, unless it causes a state of denial about their mare's conformational weaknesses. I've seen consummate horsemen make that mistake.

"So, first, realistically evaluate your mare. Determine her weaknesses so you can find a stallion that will improve on them."

He also suggests that if you can find your mare's dam and grandam, or photographs of them, they can provide valuable information. "A family of mares will present a visible tendency toward various strengths and weaknesses," he says. "For instance, if your mare has short legs, but all of her family has long legs, that suggests she may be an aberration. Her short legs are probably a problem that a long-legged stallion will easily overcome. However, if the mare's family reveals that 50 percent or more have very short legs, too, you have a challenge. A stallion with a proven history of overcoming this particular problem should be right at the top of your list."

Once you know your mare's conformational strengths and weaknesses, find a stallion that complements her strengths and helps correct her weaknesses. Short legs, long backs, necks set too low—how much can you expect a stallion to improve? There's no easy answer to that question, says George Z.

"Everything is individual. If your mare has had a foal before, study the results from that breeding to those particular bloodlines. If a mare has a strong tendency to pass on certain unfortunate characteristics, it may be hard for a stallion to overcome them. Once again, your professional evaluation will help you be realistic—one cannot ask the impossible!

Prepotency personified: Desperado V (top), owned by Don Severa and Sheila Varian, has sired scores of national champions, many, like this irresistible filly (bottom), stamped in his image. (photos by Don Severa)

"However, usually all is not lost! That is when a stallion's prepotency becomes very important. Find a stallion known for siring offspring without your mare's undesirable characteristics, and look at his offspring. Does he stamp them with his conformation regardless of the mare's bloodlines? Look for a stallion that fills a pasture with cookie-cutter images of himself. He is the sire for your foal."

George Z always asks mare owners what their goals are. "For instance, if they want Arabians and Half-Arabians with big-bodied, strong, athletic conformation, I tell them *Emanor is the one for them. If they want trot—I can report that his youngsters trot bigger than life! He is very prepotent when it comes to these characteristics. If that's what a mare owner wants, and the mare has the same athletic conformation and tendencies, then the gamble that is part of breeding horses suddenly does not seem quite so risky."

DISPOSITION

Some people will simply laugh out loud if you ask them how a stallion's disposition might impact his offspring. "What, do you think that they'll ship a little bit of his personality in that ol' Equitainer?" they'll ask, shaking their heads. Certainly, the mare that raises and nurtures her foal twenty-four hours per day has an enormous input. She teaches by example, and it's the rare foal that doesn't mimic many of his dam's personality traits.

But just as certain is the evidence that many stallions stamp their progeny with personalities similar to theirs, even though they may never meet their offspring.

One champion reining horse, Hollywood Dun It, sired offspring whose earnings surpass $4 million—an unparalleled accomplishment. Billy Powers, breeding manager at McQuay Stables in Texas, where the stallion stood, reports that every spring the pastures were filled with youngsters that executed spins and stops in the pasture almost as soon as they could walk. The stallion's prepotency for passing on his athleticism and sturdy conformation was available for the eye to see.

Just as consistent, but not so readily visible, are the even temperaments and trainable minds his offspring have. Their kind, willing dispositions have helped them achieve success in the show pen, and contributed to their value on the market. It also made Hollywood Dun It a sought-after sire in a new, somewhat unexpected market, before he passed away in March 2005.

As recently as 1990, Arabian reining horses were a scarce commodity, and Half-Arabian reiners were a real rarity. But in the dozen years that followed, a bona fide explosion in popularity has occurred—Arabian and Half-Arabian reining, as well as the Arabian Reining Horse Association are flourishing. And much of the excitement is due—if indirectly—to Hollywood Dun It.

Years ago, when the late stallion's owner, Tim McQuay, lived in Minnesota, one of his friends was Ralph Johnson, DVM. Dr. Johnson owned two purebred Arabian mares, standout athletes themselves. For many years, even after McQuay moved his operation to Texas, Dr. Johnson bred his two mares to Hollywood Dun It. Those offspring have compiled a remarkable show record.

Cory Vokoun of Buckshot Farms in Nebraska has purchased more than half a dozen of Dr. Johnson's Half-Arabians, and every one of them shown has earned at least one national reining championship. One extraordinary mare, Dun Scootin, has earned seven or eight Arabian national titles, including two in 2004, when she won the open reining with John O'Hara and the amateur class with his owner. Vokoun credits Hollywood Dun It with contributing not just physical ability to the Arabians, but also his quiet temperament.

In 2005, Half-Arabian reining captured national attention with the debut of the Half-Arabian Reining Futurity Classic at Scottsdale's big Arabian show held every February. With a payout of at least $80,000, the Classic is one of the richest National Reining Horse Association events in the country, and has spurred enormous interest. Buyers are scrambling for Half-Arabian prospects with the physical and mental aptitude for reining competition.

Arabian breeders are searching for Quarter Horse and Paint Horse sires that can complement their horses, with calm personalities that moderate the often exuberant Arabian. Some athletic stallions with "hotter" temperaments haven't done as well as the even-tempered "Dun Its." Several breeding operations, including Buckshot Farms, have purchased Hollywood Dun It sons as foundation sires for their Half-Arabian programs.

This dapper pinto Miniature Horse stallion, owned by Winsome, Etc. Miniatures, exemplifies the best of his breed. (photo by Jay Goss)

So, consider the stallion's personality, how it'll benefit the foal you plan to breed, and how it'll help you achieve your breeding goals. A horse that's a willing partner always has the edge, not just in the show pen, but as the once-in-a-lifetime "keeper," that so many horse owners seek. To breed the horse that you—and others—want to live with, remember to consider the stallion's disposition.

PEDIGREE

When you look at a horse's pedigree, you see the story of his family, their accomplishments, their history. Christie Metz, and her husband, Henry, own and operate Silver Maple Farm in Santa Ynez, California, where they breed five to nine foals per year, and stand several stallions. She's an ardent student of the history and pedigrees of every horse on their farm.

Metz, who grew up riding a Saddlebred, today breeds Arabians. She is quick to note that the Arabian, an ancient breed, has been used to provide bone density and stamina to nearly every breed around the world.

She has a particular passion for straight Egyptian and Egyptian-bred Arabians. A rare commodity, straight Egyptians represent only 3 percent of the Arabian population—good for their market, but a challenge to breeders seeking new blood for their program. It makes pedigrees, and what the past generations of horses reveal to current breeders, even more important, she says.

"When I consider breeding two individuals, the first thing I do is try to obtain pictures of the horses in their pedigrees," Metz says. She hopes for three generations, but five is even better. "Some people just look at the stallion's pedigree and neglect the mare, but all of our mares, as well as our stallions, have very strong mare lines."

(Note: When a breeder speaks of the "mare line," or "tail female" in reference to the pedigree, he or she is referring to the dam line and the individuals along the very bottom of the pedigree. Conversely, when a breeder talks about the "stallion line" or "tail male," he or she is referring to the ancestors following the sire line along the very top of the pedigree.)

By studying the horses' body structure in the pictorial pedigrees, Metz can view conformational trends, the physical traits repeatedly passed down through the generations. If it's a characteristic that appears in multiple generations and individuals, she knows there will be a strong probability it'll be passed on to the offspring.

If the characteristic is beneficial, she can rejoice, and perhaps seek a stallion with the same strong trend to accentuate it. However, if the trait isn't one she wants her foal to have, she can now look for a mate whose strengths are proven to overcome that particular weakness.

"It's very important not to breed two individuals with the same defect!" Metz states emphatically. "And be realistic, you're not going to overcome every undesirable characteristic in one generation. But you can—and should—improve with every generation."

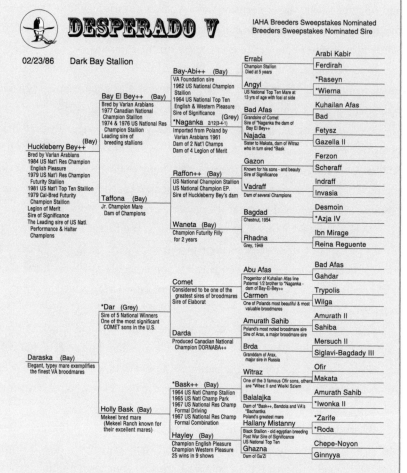

DESPERADO V

IAHA Breeders Sweepstakes Nominated
Breeders Sweepstakes Nominated Sire

02/23/86   Dark Bay Stallion

Huckleberry Bey++ (Bay)
Bred by Varian Arabians
1984 US Nat'l Res Champion
English Pleasure
1979 US Nat'l Res Champion
Futurity Stallion
1981 US Nat'l Top Ten Stallion
1979 Cal-Bred Futurity
Champion Stallion
Legion of Merit
Sire of Significance
The Leading sire of US Natl.
Performance & Halter
Champions

Bay El Bey++ (Bay)
Bred by Varian Arabians
1977 Canadian National
Champion Stallion
1974 & 1976 US National Res
Champion Stallion
Leading sire of
breeding stallions

Bay-Abi++ (Bay)
VA Foundation sire
1962 US National Champion
Stallion
1964 US National Top Ten
English & Western Pleasure
Sire of Significance

Errabi
Champion Stallion
Died at 5 years
- Arabi Kabir
- Ferdirah

Angyl
US National Top Ten Mare at
13 yrs of age with foal at side
- *Raseyn
- *Wierna

*Naganka 2/12(3-4-1) (Grey)
Imported from Poland by
Varian Arabians 1961
Dam of 2 Nat'l Champs
Dam of 4 Legion of Merit

Bad Afas
Grandsire of Comet
Sire of *Naganka the dam of
Bay El Bey++
- Kuhailan Afas
- Bad

Najada
Sister to Makata, dam of Witraz
who in turn sired *Bask
- Fetysz
- Gazella II

Taffona (Bay)
Jr. Champion Mare
Dam of Champions

Raffon++ (Bay)
US National Champion Stallion
US National Champion EP.
Sire of Huckleberry Bey's dam

Gazon
Known for his sons - and beauty
Sire of Significance
- Ferzon
- Scheraff

Vadraff
Dam of several Champions
- Indraff
- Invasia

Waneta (Bay)
Champion Futurity Filly
for 2 years

Bagdad
Chestnut, 1954
- Desmoin
- *Azja IV

Rhadna
Grey, 1949
- Ibn Mirage
- Reina Reguente

Daraska (Bay)
Elegant, typey mare exemplifies
the finest VA broodmares

*Dar (Grey)
Sire of 5 National Winners
One of the most significant
COMET sons in the U.S.

Comet
Considered to be one of the
greatest sires of broodmares
Sire of Elaborat

Abu Afas
Progenitor of Kuhailan Afas line
Paternal 1/2 brother to *Naganka -
dam of Bay-El-Bey++
- Bad Afas
- Gahdar

Carmen
One of Polands most beautiful & most
valuable broodmares
- Trypolis
- Wilga

Darda
Produced Canadian National
Champion DORNABA++

Amurath Sahib
Poland's most noted broodmare sire
Sire of Arax, a major broodmare sire
- Amurath II
- Sahiba

Brda
Granddam of Arax,
major sire in Russia
- Mersuch II
- Siglavi-Bagdady III

Holly Bask (Bay)
Mekeel bred mare
(Mekeel Ranch known for
their excellent mares)

*Bask++ (Bay)
1964 US Natl Champ Stallion
1965 US Natl Champ Park
1967 US National Res Champ
Formal Driving
1967 US National Res Champ
Formal Combination

Witraz
One of the 3 famous Ofir sons, others
are *Witez II and Wielki Szlem
- Ofir
- Makata

Balalajka
Dam of *Bask++, Bandola and VA's
*Bachantka
- Amurath Sahib
- *Iwonka II

Hayley (Bay)
Champion English Pleasure
Champion Western Pleasure
25 wins in 9 shows

Hallany Mistanny
Black Stallion - old egyptian breeding
Post War Sire of Significance
- *Zarife
- *Roda

Ghazna
Dam of Ga'zl
US National Top Ten
- Chepe-Noyon
- Ginnyya

This pedigree of the Arabian stallion Desperado V provides a wealth of information to the prospective breeder. The "top" or paternal side of the pedigree reveals that Desperado V is a fourth-generation Varian Arabian sire. His strong sire line is filled with national champions. Note: Always refer to a stallion's offspring as "by" the particular stallion. For example, *Desperado V is by Huckleberry Bey.*

The "bottom" or maternal side of the pedigree exhibits a strong tail female line, a necessity, says Cowgirl Hall of Fame inductee and top Arabian breeder, Sheila Varian. Note: Always refer to a mare's offspring as "out of" her. For example, *Desperado V is out of Daraska.* Pedigree courtesy of Varian Arabians, Arroyo Grande, California.

A pictorial pedigree, Metz adds, helps breeders develop an eye and an appreciation for anatomy, conformation, and symmetry. "Not everyone is blessed with an artist's eye, but with study, you can learn to recognize good, solid conformation. Develop a vision of what you want your foal to look like—then find a way to make it happen! Always keep your goal in mind."

When the foal arrives, all the study will be worth it, Metz says. "Nothing is more heartwarming than the minutes in the barn, right after a birth. The barn is always completely silent while the event is taking place. Then the new mother will nicker softly to her foal, and the newborn will talk back. Then, the entire barn fills with nickers and whinnies! Every horse in the barn calls out, welcoming the little one into the world—it is so cool! *It's magic.*"

Breeding & Show Record

Californian Hilda Gurney is an Olympian, a coach of dressage competitors at the highest level, and a successful horse breeder. When it comes to stallion selection, her first priority is the horse's breeding record. Has he produced top competitors himself?

"For me, it is really very simple," Gurney says. "I want to know if the stallion has sired grand prix horses, or extremely strong competitors. And I will only breed him to a mare that is so good, I want to duplicate her."

Most stallion owners will have information on hand about their horse's number of offspring, and their accomplishments in the show pen. Breed organizations and specific discipline associations are also reliable sources of data on a stallion's progeny and their performance records. (For a listing, see the resource guide.)

Successful breeders whose goal is to breed a performance horse in a certain discipline—for example, Western or English pleasure, jumping, or endurance—will seek a stallion with a proven record of siring horses that excel within that discipline.

Sue Schembri and her husband own and operate Char-O-Lot Ranch in Myckka City, Florida, and stand several world and national champion Appaloosa and Quarter Horse stallions. Among them is the aptly named The

Colonels Smokingun, "Gunner."
(photo by Cappy Jackson)

A Stallion Owner's Questions for Mare Owners

Kim Sloan, MD, and his wife, Debra, own Colonels Smokingun ("Gunner"), reining champion of the 2001 U.S. Equestrian Team Festival of Champions, National Reining Horse Association Saddlesmith open champion, and NRHA Futurity open reserve champion. Gunner is also a highly sought-after sire of reining champions.

Dr. Sloan limits breedings to his handsome overo Paint Horse stallion to fifty outside mares per year—a practice that only increases the value of the offspring. Sometimes, however, the scarcity of young Gunners, and their owner's reluctance to part with them, has made even the good doctor shake his head. In 2003, with only yearlings in his pastures at Kebra Ranch, he went looking for a three-year-old Gunner filly to buy for futurity reining competition. Alas, despite a pocket full of tempting greenbacks, that year, Dr. Sloan went without a ride.

Mare owners hoping to breed a fancy overo reining horse of their own find that their inquiries about the coveted Gunner breedings are answered, then met with questions from Dr. Sloan. He uses their response to help determine what mares will breed to his stallion.

Mare owners of all breeds and all disciplines can benefit from his insightful queries.

What do you want in a foal? "If they're just breeding for color, that's the end of the conversation," he says. "If they want a reiner or working cow horse, I have more questions for them."

What are her bloodlines; how is she bred? "Bloodlines tell a family history, and if that includes competition at the highest level, it gives the breeder good reason to hope that the foal will add to the family story."

Is your mare a performer? "Does she have a successful show record? If so, I know she probably has the conformation and trainability we'd like to see in Gunner's offspring."

Is your mare a proven producer? "If a mare has already produced an up-and-coming performer or a champion, I'd like to see her bred to my stallion."

Even after all the questions are answered, Dr. Sloan admits there is something of the unknowable in every breeding. For instance, he says, take his mare, Sidewinders Doll, who's twenty-five years old. She produced six offspring, including multiple world champions and Saddlesmith champions. One of her daughters won nine NRHA Lawson Bronzes in her reining career, and is now producing champions herself.

"If I were to evaluate her conformation, it's not the best," Dr. Sloan says. "But with a good stallion, she outproduced herself every time. As a broodmare, she is golden."

Dr. Sloan, past president of the NRHA, and Debra are both active reining competitors. They say that as stallion owners, it's a great feeling every time Gunner's offspring post a win. Is there any greater thrill? "Why, *showing* that youngster to the win, of course."

A reining champion, Gunner is a sought-after sire of champions. (photo by Cappy Jackson)

Hunter. From 2002 to 2004, The Hunter was the leading sire of world and national Appaloosa performance horses, many of them hunters.

Schembri advises would-be breeders, "Don't mix apples with oranges; stay within your chosen discipline. Understand what your mare is bred to do, either through her performance or her pedigree, then breed her with a stallion that has similar capabilities. That way, you'll double up on their talents!"

Schembri says that today there's a huge demand for hunt seat and Western pleasure horses at the upper levels of showing, and smart mare owners that breed accordingly will do well.

"But be realistic," she adds. "You normally shouldn't expect to get a 16.2-hand hunt seat champion out of a 14.2-hand broodmare. Breeding horses isn't an easy way to make money; it always must be a labor of love."

STALLION MANAGEMENT

The professionalism and reliability of the stallion's management team is an often overlooked aspect of breeding—that is, until problems arise. Savvy mare owners will do a brief but thorough investigation before they sign the breeding contract. The quality of stallion management should be an important consideration in stallion selection.

If your mare is to be bred at the stallion station, personally visit the site:

- Is it a clean, safe, healthy environment?
- Are the food and water readily available, fresh, and appetizing?
- Will your mare have daily turnout? With few exceptions, turnout is a vital ingredient to her physical and mental well-being.
- Has the staff taken equine reproductive courses? Who's handling the actual breeding, whether live cover or artificial insemination?
- Do the caregivers seem conscientious and knowledgeable? However long her stay, you want your treasured mare to remain healthy and happy.

Most breeding farms give the onsite mares preferential treatment over shipped-semen clients—determine whether this is the farm's policy. Ask how many mares they breed onsite annually, and what the conception rate is on the first breeding. Additional breedings will add to your expense.

If you're using shipped semen, learn what collection schedule the stallion uses (for example, Monday, Wednesday, and Friday) and plan accordingly with your veterinarian. Find out the stallion's first-shipment conception rate. (For additional information, see chapter 4.)

Perhaps most importantly, take the time to talk with other mare owners who've recently bred at least once to the stallion. Ask if their experience was satisfactory:

- How responsive was management to their needs?
- Were their telephone calls promptly returned?
- Were they treated courteously and professionally?
- Was semen shipped according to the stated policy of the farm?
- Would they breed their mare to that stallion again?

A well-managed stallion station can make the difference between successful breeding and abject failure. Time taken to ask key questions before you breed is time well spent.

THE STALLION OWNER'S MARKETING PROGRAM

Today, the managers of many top stallions offer special incentive programs to show and/or market the stallions' offspring. These programs can be especially important to your stallion selection if you plan to sell the foal. Financial incentives offered to owners of champion offspring benefit the stallion owners who want their stallion to gain a high-profile reputation as a successful sire, as well as the owner of the offspring.

The champion Quarter Horse stallion Zips Chocolate Chip has

A noble Morgan stallion owned by Fire Run Farm. (photo by Jay Goss)

107

had one of the most successful—and fun—stallion campaigns in history. His breeder and owner, Ann Myers, and her family, are familiar figures at big shows, dispensing delicious cookies, sometimes dressed in chocolate-chip-cookie costumes. Myers loves to say she gets inspired for new foal names while strolling her grocery store's cookie aisle. Her Web site is a chocolate-lover's dream.

The result is a "brand" with name recognition that most stallion owners only dream of. Western pleasure aficionados of all breeds have heard about Zips Chocolate Chip, which contributes to the demand for his offspring, and, in turn, the high value of his foals. Additionally, if breeders decide to sell their Chip sons or daughters, Myers accommodates them with space on her highly trafficked Web site.

Versatility plus: Jack Maritz's Arabian stallion, Thee Cyclone, was a South African national halter champion, worked sheep, and starred in the title role of Disney's *The Young Black Stallion*. Today, his offspring carry on his winning ways. (photo by Randi Clark)

When selecting a stallion, ask his managers what programs they offer. If they have a great Web site, do they offer space to clients' sale horses? Quite a few breeding farms have annual production sales. Find out whether they take consignment horses their stallions have bred. Ask whether they have a newsletter to advertise their clients' horses.

Today, many stallion owners have creative marketing programs that help clients sell their horses. If they don't, you could urge them to consider starting a program, reminding them it would reward them, too, with more breeding clients. Ask, and you might receive.

CHAPTER EIGHT

THE BREEDING CONTRACT

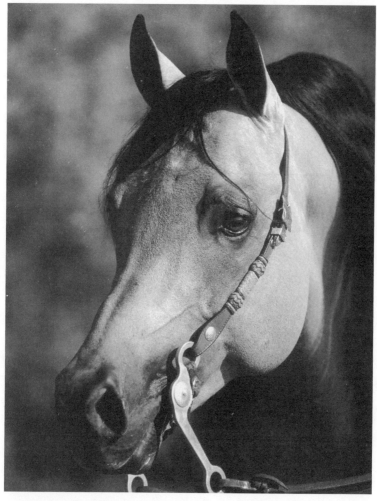

The late reining champion and superstar sire, **Hollywood Dun It,** who was owned by **McQuay/Easton.** (photo by Cappy Jackson)

UNIQUE 'CONTRACT'

During Desperado V's long breeding career, his co-owner, Sheila Varian, and I entered into hundreds of breeding contracts—but perhaps none as unique as the agreement to breed Joy Cain's two Arabian mares. It all started when Joni Otto-Smith, who worked for my architectural firm years ago, followed her interest in Native American pottery to the Santa Clara Pueblo in New Mexico.

Joni was a connoisseur of the fine pottery made by families of skilled artisans living there. Hand-coiled and naturally fired, its thick walls are polished black and carved with exquisite designs. It's sought-after by collectors and museums.

Joni met Joy Cain, a skilled potter, and her mother, Mary, who'd been featured in a National Geographic film on this special art form. It didn't take long for Joni to learn that Arabian horses were another passion of Joy's, and that she'd always dreamed of breeding her mares to Desperado V. In 2003, Joy, her mother, and other members of the family went to the National Arabian Horse Show in Albuquerque, where I met them.

I learned that Joy had carefully bred five generations of horses at her Dobrya Arabians, and how much she admired Desperado V. By the time the horse show ended, I'd offered her a breeding to Desperado V, and she, in turn, offered both Sheila and me one of her Santa Clara pots. We were all thrilled!

Unfortunately, by the following spring, Desperado's semen had diminished in quantity, and we stopped shipping it. However, Joy was quite thrilled with Sheila's generous offer to replace his breeding with two breedings to her junior stallion, Desperado V's look-alike son, MacLintock V. In 2004, Joy bred her mare.

Later, I received a note from Joy: A young neighbor of hers would be delivering my special pot. Soon afterward, late one night, there was a knock at my door. A young man, holding a large cooler, said he had something for me. A box emerged from the cooler, and from it, a glorious Santa Clara pot.

I hope that Joy is as pleased with her foal as I am with my extraordinary example of her craftsmanship. Breeding horses brings people together, and sometimes a "contract" is as unique as those individuals.

—Don Severa, Templeton, California

YOUR SPECIAL MARE IS HEALTHY, SOUND, AND A PERFECT CANdidate for producing the foal you've always dreamed of. You've narrowed the stallion selection to one or two standouts that complement your mare's strengths and improve on her weaknesses. But when the breeding contracts arrive in bulging packets in your mailbox, you wonder if a translator might not be necessary!

To assist, we've invited two of the top professionals in the horse breeding business to help us understand the fine print of breeding contracts.

Billy Powers is the breeding manager at Tim McQuay's McQuay Stables, Inc., in Tioga, Texas. Among the long line of high-profile stallions standing at McQuay Stables was the legendary sire Hollywood Dun It, whose offspring have earned in excess of $4 million; he was owned by McQuay-Easton. Today, the McQuays stand four of Hollywood Dun It's accomplished sons, and reining superstar RR Star, owned by Lundin Farm LLC.

Joe Jeane and his wife, Suzy, own and operate Down the Rail Performance Prospects in Valley View, Texas. Their stallion roster includes perennial American Quarter Horse Association leading sire Zips Chocolate Chip and his champion son, Chips Hot Chocolate, both owned by Ann Myers of Myers Horse Farms, Inc.

We'll also reprint McQuay Stables's paperwork: Powers's cover letter to potential breeding clients, their contract for onsite breeding, and their contract for shipped semen. The agreements are well thought out, concise, and cover fees, as well as a variety of potential situations. However, Powers points out, there are as many different contracts as there are breeding stallions.

As a result, both Powers and Jeane urge mare owners to review all contracts carefully. They also recommend that you interview the stallion's breeding manager for additional detailed information that applies specifically to your mare. Keep an open dialogue. Ask questions. Keep in mind that the only foolish question is the one not asked!

To give you a general idea of what to expect, note the following elements that are contained in many breeding contracts:

Booking fee.

This is usually a nonrefundable fee that represents a portion of the breeding fee and is paid at the time of signing the breeding contract.

Mare-care expenses at the stallion station.

Some mare owners may wish to bring their horse to the stallion for breeding, either by live cover or artificial insemination (AI). This is particularly

(photo by Cappy Jackson)

useful if the mare owner or the mare are new to the breeding process, or if the mare presents special challenges to a successful insemination.

Many stallion owners accommodate outside mares for varying lengths of time. Depending on the mare owner's requirements, it may be from breeding to birth. Most farms require that the mare's paperwork be in their hands in advance of her arrival at the farm. This may include copies of her registration papers, a current Coggins test (performed by a veterinarian to test for equine infectious anemia, an untreatable blood virus), a certificate of veterinary inspection, and immunization and deworming records.

Determine in advance what mare-care expenses you'll expect to pay. They may include:

- Board. Accommodation is usually computed on a daily basis; stall board is typically more expensive than pasture board. If you select stall board, ask whether your mare will have daily turnout—important to her health and well-being—and if it'll incur additional expense.

- Vitamins or supplements beyond the farm's standard issue. You may need to provide these.

- All veterinary expenses. Some farms require a cash or credit card deposit upon the mare's arrival.

- Other professional caregivers (farrier, chiropractor, acupuncturist, etc).

- Laboratory work the stallion owner may perform onsite.
- Incidentals. Ask the stallion station what additional charges to expect.

Note that if your mare is leaving the stallion station as soon as she's checked in foal, the stallion owner will normally expect your bill to be paid in full before she departs the premises, unless you've made other arrangements.

Chute fee.

Usually, this fee is applicable to mares in residence at the stallion station for breeding, and covers the stallion collection and the insemination fee. It seldom applies to clients requiring shipped semen. But to avoid confusion—ask.

Semen shipping expenses and collection schedule.

Expect a shipping and handling fee on every semen shipment. This will cover any laboratory fee, priority overnight shipping, and if necessary, rental and use of the shipping container.

With modern technology, it's an everyday occurrence for mares to be bred to stallions a mile, or a world, away. If you're using frozen semen, it may be shipped at any time and kept frozen until use. For cooled semen (used by the majority of breeders due to its higher sperm count and increased sperm vitality) tighter coordination between your mare's heat cycle and the semen shipment will be required. Cooled semen survives outside the stallion or mare only about seventy-two hours.

"To maintain the fertility of a stallion throughout a long breeding season—February 1 to August 1, in our case—most stallion owners do not collect semen on a daily basis," says Powers. "Mare owners

A Varian-bred hotshot: Chili Pepper V.
(photo by Zita)

should be aware of the collection schedule for their stallion of choice, so they and their veterinarian can plan accordingly. We collect every other day—no exceptions!

"Additionally, our first priority on any collection day is the mares at our farm to be bred," Powers adds. "They receive the semen first. So, while we do our best to honor every request for shipped semen immediately (and almost always do), we don't *guarantee* shipment on a specific day. You will find this is the case at most large breeding farms.

"We ask that mare owners send a request for semen twenty-four hours before shipping, so we can plan ahead. If they must cancel, a timely cancellation notice is necessary. I always go over all of this information with the mare owners when they sign the breeding contract, so there's no confusion."

Limitations on cooled semen shipments.

Ideally, every mare would become pregnant from the first shipment of semen. However, in the real world, on occasion another shipment is required. Check the breeding contract to see if there is a limitation on semen shipments. Some breeders have none. Others, after several shipments without a pregnancy, may require that the mare be brought to the stallion station for onsite insemination.

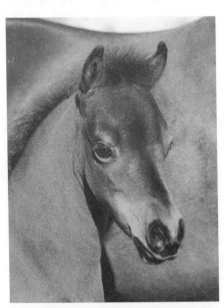

Good things come in small packages: Miniature Horse colt. (photo by Jay Goss)

Both Powers and Jeane report no limit on semen shipments, each containing one dose, and possibly, a second from extra semen. "But, after four or five shipments I may start to ask questions," Powers says. "After all, each shipment is an additional expense, and perhaps there's some advice I can offer to the attending veterinarian."

Once again, it's imperative to know the stallion owner's policy, and to keep lines of communication open between stallion manager, mare owner, and the mare's veterinarian.

Live foal guarantee.

Essentially, this is your product guarantee in the event your mare's pregnancy doesn't produce a live foal, per the definition in the breeding contract. Usually, a live foal is defined as one that stands and nurses independently. If the foal is stillborn, or if the mare aborts or absorbs after her pregnancy is confirmed, some form of rebreeding privileges are usually extended to the mare owner.

"The bottom line is we want to make sure the mare owner gets a baby," Jeane says. "We're lenient with our live foal guarantee. But you should understand your contract's specific terms because they vary from stallion to stallion, and even with one stallion, terms may change from year to year."

Live foal guarantees may include:

- A waiver or reduction of the stud fee.
- A rebreeding fee.
- Delay of the rebreeding until the following year at the stallion owner's discretion, depending on the stallion's schedule and the time of year.

Note that special rebreeding considerations of a live foal guarantee may be contingent on the mare owner performing required steps in the process:

- First, the mare owner will need to provide proof of pregnancy, either in the form of a letter from an attending veterinarian or his ultrasound picture.
- Second, the mare owner should make timely notification to the stallion manager of the loss of the foal. It is good policy to inform them of all developments.
- Additionally, if your mare has an unsuccessful pregnancy, and you decide a different mare would be a better candidate for the rebreeding, in most cases, the stallion owner's permission is required for the substitution.

Understand the specifics of your live foal guarantee and your responsibilities under it, before it becomes necessary to use it.

Paperwork.

Stallion owners everywhere agree on one thing: The enormous amount of paperwork involved in breeding is time consuming—and important. Mare owners, too, should read the breeding contract carefully, and also be aware of any paperwork they must generate.

Usually, the mare will be examined by her veterinarian and her pregnancy verified by an ultrasound scan at two and three weeks, and at one month. At one month the foal's heartbeat can be detected, and at that time, the stallion owner should be notified that a viable pregnancy is certified by the veterinarian. This record is required in the event the foal is absorbed or aborted, and the mare owner wants to activate the rebreeding privileges under the live foal guarantee.

When a beautiful baby is born, don't forget the most important paperwork of all: Notify the stallion owner promptly, after which a Breeder's Certificate will be issued, and other paperwork, breed registration, futurity nominations, etc., will be completed. (For more on the stallion-owner paperwork, see chapter 7.)

Stretching his legs at Silver Maple Farm. (photo by Darryl Larson)

Here's a copy of the January 2005 cover letter for McQuay stables.

McQuay Stables, Inc.

15135 FM 922
Tioga, TX 76271
Telephone 940-437-2470
Fax 940-437-2257

Dear Mare Owner,
Thank you for considering our stallions at McQuay Stables, Inc. Enclosed you will find information concerning our stallions, the fees, and our procedures. Please read this carefully, as it will apply to you if you will be breeding your mare to one of our stallions.

Hollywood Dun It will be standing at $10,000.00. A $1,000.00 deposit is due upon booking. The remainder is due **when your mare is 30 days in foal at our farm, or when the mare is picked up from our farm after having been exposed to the stallion.** Hollywood Dun It's book is limited to 20 SELECT MARES and Tim will approve the mares based on performance, produce records, and pedigree. All mares will be taken into consideration. If you are interested in breeding your mare to **Hollywood Dun It,** please send a copy of the mare's registration by mail, e-mail, or fax. Contracts will be sent to approved mares.

For mares not being bred to **Hollywood Dun It,** we stand four of his sons. **Dun It With A Twist** and **Reminic N Dunit for $3,000.00 before January 1, 2005, thereafter the fee is $3,500.00. Footworks Finest** and **Dun Gotta Gun will be $2,000.00.** We also stand **RR Star for $3,500.00.** Stallion fees are for onsite mares and for shipped semen mares. These fees do not include mare care, reproductive expenses, shipping expenses, or frozen semen expenses.

If your mare will be bred here at McQuay Stables, our mare care is $12 per day for pasture board and $17 per day stall board for a wet or dry mare. All mares arriving prior to April 15 will be under lights and on stall board until they are at least 14 days in foal. We require from our mare owners a current (within one year) Coggins, a veterinary health certificate, a photo static copy (both sides) of the papers, and any immunization and worming records you have for the mare. AS OF THE 2001 BREEDING SEASON, ALL MARE OWNERS WILL BE REQUIRED TO MAKE A $200 DEPOSIT PER MARE, OR AUTHORIZED USE OF A CREDIT CARD

TO COVER VETERINARY EXPENSES. If all veterinary expenses are kept current we will refund the $200 or disregard the credit card authorization. Past experience of both McQuay Stables and our veterinarian (Equine Medical Associates) has left us with this decision. All mare owners will be required to sign a breeding contract and a client contract. No alterations or exceptions will be acceptable. Your mare will not be accepted if McQuay Stables does not receive both contracts prior to, or upon her arrival. NO MARE WILL BE PERMITTED TO LEAVE MCQUAY STABLES PRIOR TO ALL SERVICES BEING PAID IN FULL TO BOTH MCQUAY STABLES AND EQUINE MEDICAL ASSOCIATES.

If your mare will be bred using shipped semen the stallion fee must be paid 10 days prior to the first shipment. There will be no exceptions. For EACH shipment from McQuay Stables there will be a shipping fee of $150.00 to the mare owner. This fee includes Federal Express priority overnight service and counter-to-counter air transport service. Because the $150.00 charge applies EACH time the semen is shipped, it is imperative that your veterinarian be aware of your mare's current breeding status and be confident that she is, in fact, ready to be bred. **Have your vet contact McQuay Stables at least 24 hours prior to when they will need semen for your mare.** This will help us plan for your potential needs for semen. **ALL REQUESTS FOR SEMEN MUST BE MADE BY 5:00 P.M. (Central Time) THE DAY BEFORE A BREEDING DAY.** Saturdays, Sundays, and holidays included. Please remember that shipped semen is based on availability. Semen may only be requested for regularly scheduled breeding days (every other day). Contact the farm for each specific month's breeding days (odd or even days). Stallions will not be collected on a NON-BREEDING DAY. No exceptions will be made.

McQuay Stables requires all mare owners to call during normal business hours (Monday–Friday 8 A.M.–5 P.M.) **at least two days prior to picking up their mare.** After your mare has been settled with shipped semen it is the mare owner's responsibility to contact McQuay Stables to inform us that your mare is in foal PRIOR TO OCTOBER 1st. You must also call us when your mare has foaled. At this time we will issue a Breeder's Certificate.

Please read the enclosed information carefully. Let us know if you have any questions. We look forward to hearing from you.

Sincerely,
Billy J. Powers
Breeding Manager
McQuay Stables, Inc.

On-Site Stallion Service Contract
Estimated date of mare's arrival

15135 E FM 922 ♦ Tioga, TX 76271 ♦ (940) 437-2470 FAX (940) 437-2257 ♦ mcquaystables@direcway.com ♦ www.mcquaystables.com

I hereby agree on ____ day of _____ to breed the mare, _____

registration number _____ , to the stallion, _____

registration number _____ , for the _____ breeding season.

1. The stallion fee is $_____ which includes a non-refundable booking fee of $_____ which is payable at the time this contract is signed and returned. The balance of the stallion fee must be paid upon billing when the mare is pronounced safe in foal, or when the mare is picked up from the Stallion Manager having been exposed to the stallion.

2. Upon arrival, the mare will be in healthy and sound breeding and physical condition and will be free from infections, contagious, or transmittable disease. A current (within 1 year) Coggins test, a copy of the mares registration papers, and a veterinarian's health certificate will accompany the mare at the time of delivery to the Stallion Manager or the MARE WILL NOT BE PERMITTED ON THE PROPERTY.

3. The mare owner agrees to pay $300.00, if applicable, to have the mare foal on the premises of the Stallion Manager. This will include foaling out the mare and initial inoculation and antibiotics administered to the foal. All other veterinary expenses incurred in connection with the foaling shall be paid by the Mare Owner.

4. The Stallion Manager agrees to provide suitable facilities for the care and feed of the mare and foal (if applicable). Mare Owner agrees to pay for the care and feed at a rate of $12.00 per day for pasture board, or $17.00 per day for stall board. This applies to both a wet or dry mare.

5. Mare Owner agrees to pay a $50.00 chute fee for non-resident mares. The chute fee will apply each time the mare is inseminated and shall be paid directly to the farm. Mare Owner agrees to pay a $25.00 pick up fee on all semen picked up at the farm.

6. The Stallion Manager will exercise reasonable judgment in the care and supervision of the mare and foal (if applicable). Stallion Manager's veterinarian, Equine Medical Associates, Inc. will examine the mare for normal breeding conditions and will administer mare care as deemed necessary for the health and safety of the mare and foal (if applicable). All veterinarian expenses will be paid by the Mare Owner directly to the veterinarian.

7. The Mare Owner agrees to assume all risk of death, sickness, or injury to the mare, except such harm as may be caused by the grossly negligent or reckless conduct of the Stallion Manager, its agents or employees.

8. The Stallion Manager agrees to use their reasonable best efforts to settle the owner's mare. The Mare Owner agrees to give the Stallion Manager ample opportunity to settle the mare, which shall include the opportunity to breed the mare through at least two (2) heat cycles. The breeding season ends July 15th.

9. This contract contains a "Live Foal Guarantee". If the mare leaves the Stallion Manager's property prior to her 30 day pregnancy check the "Live Foal Guarantee" will be void. A Live foal is described as a newborn foal which stands and nurses without assistance. If a foal is born dead, or the mare absorbs/aborts a predetermined pregnancy there are return privileges, only if the Stallion Manager is notified within thirty (30) days and receives a statement confirming this.

10. If the mare absorbs or aborts a pregnancy after having been pregnancy checked in foal, or if the mare fails to conceive during the normal breeding season, the Stallion Manager agrees to breed the same mare again during the immediately following year's breeding season. There is a charge of $250.00 for re-breed service expenses. A substitute mare, accepted by the Stallion Manager, may be sent ONLY if the original mare is deceased or deemed unfit for breeding.

11. A Breeder's Certificate will be issued for the foal conceived as a result of the breeding. The Breeder's Certificate will be issued only after all breeding and veterinary expenses have been paid in full and after the foal is born and has been reported to the Stallion Manager.

12. The parties acknowledge that this agreement is made and shall be considered to be entirely performed within the State of Texas and shall be construed and enforced under the laws of the State of Texas Law (Chapter 87, civil practice and remedies code), an equine professional is not liable for an injury or death of a participant in equine activities resulting from the inherent risks of equine activities.

13. When signed by both parties this document will become a legally enforceable contract binding upon both parties. The Mare Owner hereby grants the Stallion Manager a lien upon the mare and foal (if applicable) for any unpaid stallion fees, mare care charges, veterinary expenses, and any other charges resulting from the mare being on the Stallion Manager's premises.

Mare Owner _____
                        Printed Name

Mare Owner _____   Stallion Manager _____
                        Signature   Tim McQuay

Mare Owner Address: _____

_____

Telephone Number: _____ Fax Number: _____ Email: _____

McQuay Stables

Cooled Transported Contract

15135 E FM 922 ♦ Tioga, TX 76271 ♦ (940) 437-2470 FAX (940) 437-2257 ♦ mcquaystables@direcway.com ♦ www.mcquaystables.com

I hereby agree on ____ day of _____ to breed the mare, _____

registration number _____ , to the stallion, _____

registration number _____ , using cooled, transported semen for the _____ breeding season.

1. The stallion fee for cooled transported semen is _____. This includes the _____ non-refundable booking fee which is payable upon execution of the contract. There is a $150 charge per shipment for shipping expenses. The remainder of the stallion fee and the first shipping charge are due ten (10) days prior to shipment or the semen will not be sent.
2. A photostatic copy, both sides, of the registration papers on your mare must accompany this contact. The owner recorded on the registration certificate will be the owner recorded on the stallion breeding report.
3. Mares on the premises of McQuay Stables, Inc.'s have a breeding priority on any given breeding day. Therefore, we make no guarantee that cooled semen will be available for transportation on any specific day.
4. McQuay Stables, Inc. collects stallions on an Every-Other-Day Basis. We Will Not Make Exceptions! This is to preserve stallion fertility throughout our breeding season. McQuay Stables, Inc.'s breeding season exists February 1st through August 1st.
5. A request for a shipment of cooled transported semen must be made at least 24 hours prior to shipping time. Cancellation must be made by 7:30 am (Central Time) shipping day. Failure to cancel by 7:30 am (Central Time) will result in a $150 shipping charge. Cancellations can be made by telephone, fax, and e-mail messages. Semen will only be sent via counter-to-counter air transport services. (American Air, United Air, Delta Air, and Northwest Air) or by FED-EX.
6. This contract contains a "Live Foal Guarantee". A live foal is described as a newborn foal which stands and nurses without assistance. If a foal is born dead, or the mare absorbs/aborts a predetermined pregnancy there are return privileges, only if the Stallion Manager is notified within thirty (30) days and receives a statement confirming this. A "Live Foal Guarantee" will apply only to those mares that are certified in foal by a licensed, attending veterinarian. Confirmation of such pregnancy in the form of documented ultrasound picture or letter from the attending veterinarian must be received by October 1 of the breeding year or the mare will not be included in the Stallion Breeding Report.
7. If the mare absorbs or aborts a pregnancy after having been pregnancy checked in foal, or if the mare fails to conceive during normal breeding season, the Stallion Manager agrees to breed the same mare again during the immediately following year's breeding season. There is a charge of $250 for re-breed service expenses. A substitute mare, accepted by the Stallion Manager, may be used ONLY if the original mare is deceased or deemed unfit for breeding by an accredited veterinarian.
8. A Breeder's Certificate will be issued for the foal conceived as a result of the breeding. The Breeder's Certificate will be issued only after all expenses have been paid in full and after the foal is born and has been reported to the Stallion Manager.
9. Neither McQuay Stables, Inc. nor any of its officers or employees shall be liable for damages as a result of damage to the semen or as a result of a mare failing to settle. McQuay Stables, Inc.'s sole liability under this contract is in the event the stallion should die or become unfit for breeding purposes this contract shall terminate and any money paid on the stallion fee, except the non-refundable booking fee, shall be refunded to the Mare Owner.
10. When signed by both parties this document will become a legally enforceable contract, binding upon both parties. The parties acknowledge that this agreement is made and shall be considered to be entirely performed within the State of Texas and shall be construed and enforced under the laws of the State of Texas Law (Chapter 87, civil practice and remedies code), and equine professional is not liable for an injury or death of a participant in equine activities resulting from the inherent risks of equine activities.

Mare Owner _____
                        Printed Name

Mare Owner _____   Stallion Manager _____
                        Signature   Tim McQuay

Mare Owner Address: _____

_____

Telephone Number: _____ Fax Number: _____ Email: _____ Mare Owner

PART TWO

THE NEXT
ELEVEN MONTHS

Perfect light, lovely sight! Varian Arabians. (photo by Zita)

CHAPTER NINE

BROODMARE CARE

(photo by Cappy Jackson)

First-Time Jitters

It was a happy decision. When we moved to our new horse property, I picked up my Arabian mare, Fantasia, from the boarding barn for the last time, and brought her home to my backyard. Then I decided she could use a pasture-mate—why not the foal of my dreams?

Fantasia was a maiden mare, and it was my first time to breed a horse. I knew nothing about it! But I did my research and met a breeder nearby who became my mentor. She also owned a champion pinto Half-Arabian stallion that I thought would be a terrific mate for my mare. I didn't care about the color—I just wanted a healthy foal, a keeper.

Fantasia had a perfect pregnancy. When her foaling date was near, she started to "wax up" and show other signs of impending birth. I awoke one morning, looked at my mare, knew she was about to foal, and felt totally inadequate to help her if anything went wrong. I totally panicked.

I called the stallion owner to tell her I was bringing Fantasia to her farm, saying, "We're on the road, about an hour away, and if she starts giving birth in the trailer—come find us!"

We made it to her farm. In fact, Fantasia waited until the next day to produce a flawless tobiano buckskin filly. I was glad we were there, because I learned from my friend's experience, and Fantasia certainly had better care than I would've provided alone.

It was such an extraordinary experience, both the birth and raising a foal, that a couple of years later I bred another mare to the same stallion. She was a veteran broodmare, and I'd attended several additional births, so I planned to foal her out at home. I was confident I could handle it.

When she was ready to give birth, I set my alarm every half hour for three nights . . . but no foal. On the third morning, I fed her, then went inside for some breakfast. When I returned to the barn twenty minutes later, the baby, a buckskin colt, was born, and the mare was up!

Two different foaling experiences—both unforgettable—followed by the unique joy of raising and training the babies I'd so carefully planned. Chantilly Lace and Charizmatic Gold have a permanent place in my heart—and my barn!

—Cheryl Ginder, Olympic Peninsula, Washington

IN A NORMAL PREGNANCY, YOUR MARE'S GESTATION PERIOD will be from 325 to 365 days. One calculation trick is to think, "one year minus three weeks." Here, we've broken down the gestation period into four parts: Days 0 to 100; Days 101 to 200; Days 201 to 300; and Day 301 to Term. We'll first give you a broodmare-care program to optimize the health of both your mare and her growing fetus. (Note: This chapter will address healthy broodmare care only; for potential pregnancy problems, see Chapter 10.) Then we'll tell you what to expect in terms of fetal development and what special care she'll need during each stage.

Our mare-care expert is Barb Crabbe, DVM, who breeds, boards, and foals out broodmares at her thirty-two-acre Pacific Crest Sporthorse in Oregon City, Oregon; plus, she oversees about thirty to forty equine-patient foalings per year.

OVERALL CARE

While your mare is pregnant, there are a few overall do's and don'ts to keep in mind:

- Do keep up your mare's routine maintenance, including deworming, farrier work, and grooming. (For details, see chapter 3.)
- Don't have any dental work performed. The heavy sedation and bacterial exposure can compromise fetus health. If you breed your mare every year, be sure to have dental work done right after she foals, in the brief window of time between pregnancy and re-breeding. If you're a first-time breeder, just be sure you have your mare's dental work done before you breed your mare.
- Don't give your mare a feed-through fly-control product. There's documentation that feeding a pregnant mare such a product—which is actually a toxin—can cause problems with fetal development.
- Do feel free to trailer your mare reasonable distances, if you need to and she's used to it. You might need to trailer her to and from the stallion's farm if you opt for live cover, or to a foaling station as she nears term. Such travel is fine, as long as she's not unduly stressed (see below).

- Don't stress your mare any more than you have to, especially for the first forty-five days. When she's stressed, her body releases *cortisol*—a stress-related hormone. If she has too much cortisol in her blood-stream, it can affect fetal development and can lead to embryonic loss/abortion.

- Don't introduce a new sport or activity to your mare. For instance, don't begin training or conditioning her for a new sport or activity. If you're already going on long trail rides, or your mare is a four-foot hunter, go ahead and continue engaging in these activities; just don't start a routine your mare isn't used to.

- Do avoid fescue hay and pastures. Fescue is often plagued by a fungus, *Acremonium coenophialum,* which can cause mares to abort or hold pregnancies too long. It also affects mammary-gland development. (For details, see chapter 10.)

- Do aim for a Henneke Body-Condition Index of 5 to 6 when your mare is in her early to midpregnancy and a score of 6 to 7 while she's in her late pregnancy. (See chapter 3.)

- Do minimize your mare's exposure to other horses to reduce risk of her catching a virus. Especially dangerous are *EHV-1* (equine herpesvirus-1, subtype 1; a subtype of equine viral rhinopneumonitis also known as "viral herpes abortion") and *EHV-4* (equine herpesvirus-4, a subtype of equine viral rhinopneumonitis also known as the "respiratory rhino virus"). Herpes can lead to spontaneous abortion. (For details, see chapter 10.)

- Do call your veterinarian if you see any vaginal discharge during your mare's pregnancy; it could be a sign of *placentitis* (an infection of the placenta).

VACCINATIONS/MEDICATIONS

During your mare's pregnancy, there are certain infectious diseases for which your veterinarian will vaccinate only if the diseases are common in your area. These include anthrax, botulism, leptospirosis, strangles, and salmonella. In general, these vaccinations aren't recommended for pregnant mares.

Don't vaccinate, period, in the first ninety days. Although veterinarian opinions vary on this blanket edict, what's certain is that vaccinations stimulate the mare's immune system, which can negatively affect the unborn foal. In other words, the mare's immune system creates antibodies that could attack the developing fetus, causing a spontaneous abortion.

Following is a list of vaccinations and drugs to avoid or minimize the first hundred days to ensure the health of the fetus.

- Avoid West Nile virus vaccine.
- Avoid using TMS-SMZ (an antibiotic), unless recommended by your veterinarian. (Although there are some risks involved, this antibiotic is best for treating placentitis.)
- Avoid using phenylbutazone ("bute"), unless recommended by your veterinarian. Bute crosses the placental barrier, and can raise the risk of gastric ulcers in the future foal.

For recommended vaccinations during your mare's pregnancy, see the development breakdown on the following pages.

DEWORMING PROGRAM

For the first three hundred days, you'll follow your mare's normal deworming routine, whether that entails an *interval-* or *daily deworming program.* Both deworming types interrupt a worm's life cycle. Briefly, your mare ingests worm larvae that live in her manure and contaminate her feed in her pasture and/or stall. Once ingested, some larvae types (such as large and small strongyles) migrate through her body tissues and settle into her intestines, where they mature and lay eggs. Your mare then passes these eggs in her manure, where they hatch into larvae and spread throughout her living quarters. She ingests the larvae, and the cycle is repeated.

An interval (purge) deworming program kills adult worms in your mare's gut *before* they have a chance to lay eggs. With this type of deworming program, some veterinarians suggest that you rotate classes of dewormers so the worms won't be able to build resistance to any one class; others—such as Dr. Crabbe—do not. Discuss rotational deworming programs with your veterinarian.

A direct youngster at Bath Brothers Quarter Horses, Laramie, Wyoming.
(photo by Heidi Nyland)

A daily deworming program, on the other hand, kills worm larvae before they migrate through your mare's body tissues, thus minimizing damage.

Note that you'll need to give your mare additional dewormers to kill such parasites as bots, tapeworms, and encysted cyathostomes (a type of immature small strongyles), and roundworms. As you prepare for foaling, you'll especially zero in on roundworms. (For details, see "Day 300 to Term.")

Managing your mare's internal parasites will:

Provide optimal nutrition to your mare.

Internal parasites rob your mare of essential nutrients.

Provide optimal nutrition to the developing fetus.

Anything that happens to your mare, nutritionally speaking, also affects her fetus.

Help prevent colic.

Body-tissue damage caused by worm larvae can cause colic. Colic in pregnant mares can lead to *endotoxemia* (toxins released into the bloodstream, causing hemorrhages, kidney failure, and shock). There's also the possibility of colic surgery, which means you'd risk exposing the developing foal to anesthesia. (For details, see chapter 10.)

Reduce the parasite load in the environment.

The fewer internal parasites your mare carries, the fewer will wind up in her manure—thus, her pasture and/or stall. By cutting down the parasite population in your mare's environment, you'll reduce your foal's exposure to parasites after birth.

NUTRITIONAL PROGRAM

"I don't change the mare's nutritional intake in the early stages of pregnancy," Dr. Crabbe says. "Just make sure she's already getting a balanced diet. Of course, this also includes unlimited access to a salt/mineral block and fresh, clean water."

By providing your mare with a balanced ration, you'll not only help keep her healthy, you'll also help nourish the developing fetus. A malnourished mare—and fetus—can result in abnormal fetal development, and even abortion.

There's no one nutritional program that will work for pregnant mares in all regions of the country. For one thing, the mineral content in the soil around the country in which forage is grown differs. If the soil in your area is deficient in, say, zinc or copper, you'll need to balance out that deficiency with supplements.

Have your forage tested by your local extension service or feed company to see whether it's deficient in any minerals, and to evaluate its value for protein and digestibility. Then discuss your mare's nutrition and rations with your veterinarian.

Iodine is an important mineral to the health of your pregnant mare and her developing fetus; deficiencies can lead to problems. You might need to add an iodine supplement to your mare's feed.

Also, pay close attention to the selenium level in your forage. This essential mineral has a *narrow toxicity range*—that is, you need to make sure your mare is getting enough for optimal health, but too much can lead to problems, including birth defects in her foal. As with other minerals, selenium levels depend on the soil in which your mare's forage is grown. Your mare's forage might be selenium deficient, in which case you'd need to feed your mare a supplement; or it could provide too much of the mineral. (Note that a blood test will also determine if your mare is getting the correct amount of selenium.) If your mare's selenium level is off, consult with your veterinarian.

At about eight months into your mare's pregnancy, increase her protein and calcium intake to ensure proper fetal development and to provide her with enough nutrients to *lactate* (produce milk). Specifically:

- Increase the protein makeup of your mare's daily intake to 14 percent.
- If you feed grass hay, supply your mare with a 2:1 calcium-to-phosphorous ratio; if you feed legume hay, supply her with a 1:1 calcium-to-phosphorous ratio. (Legume hay has a higher calcium content than grass hay.)
- Consider alfalfa hay. "Alfalfa hay is a great source of protein and calcium," Dr. Crabbe notes. "Our pregnant mares get a flake of alfalfa a day."
- Increase feeding frequency. As the fetus grows, your mare's uterus is pushed into her stomach, creating less room there. Frequent feedings will keep her digestive system active, reducing colic risk.

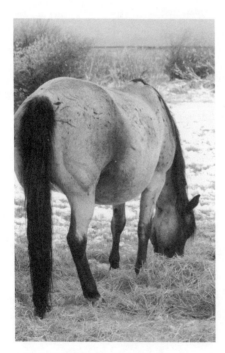

(photo by Heidi Nyland)

To implement this program, again, have your forage tested, and discuss any supplementations with your veterinarian.

Note that your mare should gain 14.5 percent of her body weight in the last three months of her pregnancy, which takes into account her fetus, fluids, etc. For example, if she normally weighs 1,000 pounds, she should weigh about 1,145 pounds. You can estimate her weight with a weight tape; your veterinarian will also evaluate your mare's weight and condition during general pregnancy examinations. If she doesn't weigh enough, increase her calories by providing grain supplementation, on your vet's advice. On the flip side, note that excessive weight gain can lead to founder.

EXERCISE ROUTINE

The amount of exercise you ask of your pregnant mare all depends on her. "Pay attention—listen to your mare," says Dr. Crabbe. "She'll tell you if she's uncomfortable with exercise."

If your pregnant mare is young, healthy, and energetic, you might be able to exercise her—both in-hand and under saddle—almost right up to foaling time. On the other hand, an aged broodmare will need a bit more pampering. Use your common sense.

In any case, it's important for your mare to get out and get moving to maintain optimal circulation and muscle tone. She'll need muscles to push out her foal. Turn her out as much as possible, weather permitting. If she objects to the saddle, ride her bareback or hand-walk her. Do some groundwork exercises to keep her mentally challenged.

If you normally show your mare, continue to do so until she seems uncomfortable with what you ask of her. But be careful: The more you expose her to other horses, the greater her risk for contracting EHV-1 and/or EHV-4, described earlier. Vaccines aren't 100 percent effective.

One cautionary note: Exertion can cause fatigue of the muscles in your mare's perineum, which can then lead to *wind-sucking*, or aspiration of air into a mare's vagina. This, in turn, can lead to infection. If you plan to regularly work your pregnant mare—such as in performance events—consider Caslick's surgery, in which her vulva is partially sutured. (See chapter 6.)

UDDER CHECK

Some mares—especially maiden mares—take exception to having their udders handled, so start accustoming your mare to having her udder handled as soon as you can in the pregnancy. You'll need to be able to handle her udder to check waxing and secretions, and to clean her udder prior to foaling, so

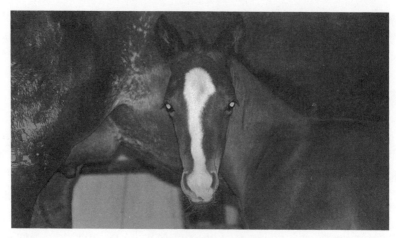

(photo by Heidi Nyland)

the foal will have clean teats on which to suck. This process will also ready your mare to the feel of her foal approaching her udder and nursing.

Here's how to safely handle your mare's udder.

Safe handling.

Don't simply walk up to your mare and put your face up to the udder area, or you could get kicked in the face. *You don't have to look at the udder in order to handle it.* Keep your face turned away. "People think their mares won't kick them, but they will," notes Dr. Crabbe. "And they'll kick hard and fast." Instead, follow these steps.

- Outfit your mare in a halter and a twelve-foot lead rope. Don't tie her, as she might panic and pull back, which can lead to stress or even an injury. This is the last thing you want to have happen, both for her sake and that of the fetus.
- Begin by approaching your mare from the left. Hold the lead rope in your left hand, and stand at her shoulder facing her flank.
- If your mare seems balky at any point in this process—that is she pins her ears, swishes her tail, or threatens to kick—position her so that her right side is against a stall or aisle wall, so she'll have less room to maneuver. If she's especially balky, ask a knowledgeable horseperson to hold her. You might even need to use a humane twitch or a

132

makeshift rope one. (If you've never used a twitch before, again, ask for help from a knowledgeable horseperson.) Keep in mind that your mare's pregnancy might affect her mood in unpredictable ways, even if she's normally easy to work around.

- Depending on the length of your arms, rest your left elbow or forearm on your mare's flank. That way, you'll be able to detect subtle signs— such as a body-weight shift—of an impending kick. If you feel such a sign, bring your hand up to her flank and try again. "I've been kicked terribly in the knees when I wasn't paying attention," says Dr. Crabbe.
- With your right hand, slowly run your hand down her belly, until you reach the udder. If she balks, slow down. If you can't get your hand down to her udder on the first day without her showing signs of an impending kick, stop on a good note and try again the following day.
- When your reach the udder, at first, you'll simply handle and massage the udder and udder area. Later, you'll extract milk from the udder, and as foaling time nears, you'll thoroughly clean the area.
- Switch sides and repeat this process—after all, her foal will be nursing on both sides!

Secretion check.

When your mare *bags up* (that is, her udders begin to enlarge) you can express the fluid. Mares bag up an average of six weeks prior to foaling. "I check milk secretions every couple of days when I begin to get it out," says Dr. Crabbe. "Udder development really varies. Experienced broodmares may have something in there all the time, while maidens wait until the last minute. Some only bag up days before foaling. The average is probably two to three weeks prior to foaling." The secretion starts out clear and sticky— kind of a honey color. It begins to turn thin and white—like skim milk—as foaling approaches.

Once the milk turns white, you can start to check it for calcium levels—a pretty good predictor of time of foaling, according to Dr. Crabbe. "We check calcium levels once the milk starts to turn white," she says. "We'll check it every other day, initially, then every day when the levels begin increasing. Once the levels get to 200 parts per million or 40 milligrams per deciliter, we start overnight monitoring, because foaling is likely within forty-eight hours.

(photo by Zita)

The test is very reliable." For simplicity, you can use test strips made for this purpose (such as the Predict-A-Foal kit, available from animal-health-product suppliers).

To get the milk out, wash your hands, and follow the safe handling directions, above. Once you reach the udder, place your hand between the teats and massage the area. Pretend you're milking a cow. Grasp the udder first, then draw your fingers down along the teat to try to draw out the fluid. If you don't get any fluid, your mare might not be producing any, or you might not be milking her correctly. If you need to, ask a knowledgeable person to help you.

About twenty-four hours prior to foaling, your mare might *wax up*; that is, a bit of discharge might accumulate at the tips of her teats.

Mastitis check.

If your mare's udder feels swollen and hard, don't automatically assume that she has *mastitis* (an infection of the udder). As your mare gets closer to foaling, her udder might feel large and hard as it fills with milk—that's normal. To check for mastitis, take her temperature and monitor her udder secretions. (For how to take your mare's temperature, see chapter 10.) If her temperature is elevated (above 101.5 degrees Fahrenheit) *and* her secretions are foul-smelling or clumpy—rather than thick and clear, or thin and whitish— she might have mastitis; call your veterinarian immediately.

Udder cleaning.

When it's time to clean your mare's udder, which you'll do daily when foaling seems imminent, first wash your hands thoroughly. Then prepare a clean washcloth and warm water. Avoid using soap or any other chemicals, which can irritate her skin—and isn't really necessary. And avoid using any toxins, such as fly spray. Such toxins can harm your foal when ingested. Follow the safe-handling procedure outlined earlier. Once you reach the udder, thoroughly wash the udder and udder area.

DAYS 0–100

Fetal development:

After fertilization, a *zygote* (fertilized egg) will form and will turn into an embryo. By about Day 6, the embryo will drop from the oviduct into the uterus. At about Day 8 to 10—or 15 to 16 days after conception—the embryo will find a place to attach itself. At Day 28, your veterinarian will be able to detect a fetal heartbeat.

"You probably won't see too much difference in your mare at this stage," says Dr. Crabbe. "Although most pregnant mares will stop cycling, don't be alarmed if yours shows signs of heat. Some mares will demonstrate signs of heat even when they are pregnant. If your mare does come into heat, however, go ahead and schedule an appointment with your veterinarian for an ultrasound scan to confirm her pregnancy. On the other hand, don't assume she's pregnant just because she isn't cycling. It's possible she's simply shutting down for winter anestrus, especially if you've bred her later in the season.

"In terms of mood," continues Dr. Crabbe, "you might notice that your mare is becoming mellow, due to the release of the hormone progesterone. She might also become grumpy at some point. There's a theory that such grumpiness can be caused by development of gonads, that is, the male reproductive organs, and the related hormonal release in a male fetus."

When will your mare start to show? It's highly variable. A maiden mare might not look pregnant until just before she foals—or even then. An older broodmare might look pregnant all the time. "It depends on the mare's body type, how many foals she's had, and her condition," says Dr. Crabbe.

Fetal size:

At Day 6, the embryo isn't quite visible to the naked eye; it's smaller than a grain of salt. By Day 25, it's the size of an ant; by Day 100, it's the size of a kitten.

Veterinary checkup.

- *General examination.*
- *Ultrasound.* Your veterinarian will want to perform an ultrasound scan to check your mare at Day 14 and Day 28. At Day 14, your vet will check for a live embryo; he or she will also check for twins. At Day 28, your vet will check for a heartbeat (you'll be able to see the flutter on the ultrasound screen) to make sure your mare is carrying a live embryo, and will check again for twins. (Sometimes, only one embryo is visible on Day 14, when actually two are present.) Depending on your vet's preference and judgment, this might be the end of the ultrasound checkups for your mare. (If you have a problem mare, your vet may want to check on her more often; for details, see chapters 6 and 10.)

  Checking for twins at Day 14 is ideal, before the embryo (or embryos) is fixed in the uterus. It roams around until Day 16. If there are two viable embryos, one can be easily crushed (or reduced) at this stage, especially if they're in opposite uterine horns. If they're in the same horn, the second embryo will likely self-reduce (die on its own), unless it's aligned in a certain way that allows it to continue to grow. This alignment—which would allow your mare to carry the twins to term—happens 10 percent of the time.

  If twins are detected, some veterinarians prefer to wait until Day 28 to see if one will self-reduce, because of the risk that you might lose both embryos in the process of crushing one. First, there's the risk you might crush both embryos. Or, you might lose both embryos in the fluid that's released during the crushing process. (For details on the risks of allowing your mare to carry—or attempt to carry—twins to term, see chapter 10.)

  Tip: Check your stallion contract; some contracts require that you have your mare regularly checked at specific times during the pregnancy.

- *Vaccinations.* On Day 90, your veterinarian *might* give your mare an EHV-1 ("rhino") vaccination; it'll be up to him or her. As noted, this will help prevent your mare from contracting equine herpesvirus-1, which can cause spontaneous abortion.

(photo by Cappy Jackson)

Days 101–200

Fetal development:

"By Day 101, the fetus is a pretty formed little guy," says Dr. Crabbe. "It looks like a horse, and has bones, hooves, etc. By Day 200, it's getting mane and tail hairs, and the sex is clearly visible."

Fetal size:

By Day 200, the fetus is the size of a pygmy goat.

Veterinary checkup.

- *General examination.*
- *Ultrasound.* Your veterinarian might recommend another ultrasound scan if you have an "at risk" mare (such as an aged mare, or one that's aborted in the past), or she exhibits any signs of abnormalities, such as vaginal discharge. At this stage, pregnancy can generally be confirmed just with a rectal palpation. Your vet will likely wish to confirm your mare's pregnancy before giving the first EHV-1 ("rhino") vaccination and beginning other pregnant-mare management routines, outlined on the following pages.

- *Vaccinations.* Once pregnancy is confirmed, your veterinarian will give your mare an EHV-1 ("rhino") vaccination on Day 150. As noted, this will help prevent your mare from contracting equine herpesvirus-1, which can cause spontaneous abortion.

DAYS 201–300

Fetal development:

During this time, the fetus mostly just gets bigger; this is why optimal nutrition is so important. It'll look like a foal by Day 300, and no wonder, as at that point it's just twenty-five days away from what's considered "normal gestation."

Fetal size:

By Day 300, the fetus is the size of a Great Dane—almost a foal!

Veterinary checkup.

- *General examination.*
- *Vaccinations.* On Day 210, your veterinarian will give your mare another EHV-1 ("rhino") vaccination. As noted, this will help prevent your mare from contracting equine herpesvirus-1, which can cause spontaneous abortion.

DAYS 301 TO TERM

Fetal development:

Between Day 300 and term, the fetus simply continues to grow. It finishes getting its haircoat, and its lungs prepare to breathe.

Fetal size:

Just about foal size!

Veterinary checkup.

- *General examination.*

- *Prefoaling procedures.* Between Day 310 and 320, your veterinarian will open any Caslick's sutures (see chapter 6), and give you a general consultation on foaling procedures.

- *Vaccinations.* At the same time, your veterinarian will give your mare a full spectrum of intramuscular vaccinations, including those for tetanus, encephalitis (also known as sleeping sickness; depending on where you live, this vaccination will include the Western equine, Eastern equine, and/or Venezuelan equine varieties), equine influenza, equine viral rhinopneumonitis, and West Nile virus; optional vaccinations include those for equine monocytic erhlichiosis (Potomac horse fever) and rabies.

  Note that vaccinations given must be *intramuscular* (administered directly into the muscle tissue), rather than *intranasal* (administered via the membranes in the nose) for such diseases as influenza and strangles. Intramuscular vaccines stimulate an antibody response, meaning that they stimulate your mare to produce antibodies, which are then transferred to the colostrum so the foal will get protection. Intranasal vaccines stimulate only a local immune response, which doesn't affect the colostrum. Antibodies in the colostrum will help protect your foal from infectious disease for up to twelve months.

  "By fully vaccinating your mare thirty days prior to foaling, you'll stimulate antibodies in your mare's bloodstream that will then transfer to her colostrum or first milk," Dr. Crabbe says. "Note that unlike some species, mares pass all the antibodies to their foals in the colostrum; nothing is passed through the placenta. That's why it's so important that your newborn foal gets his full share of colostrum."

- *Deworming:* In addition to your normal deworming routine, plan to deworm your mare with fenbendazole (brand name, Panacur Power Pak) as close to foaling as possible. This is a five-day regimen of a double dose of fenbendazole that kills parasite larvae, so it'll do a complete cleanout. Try to plan this deworming program so that the fifth day of deworming falls on the day of foaling.

  This dewormer kills *strongyloides westeri* (roundworm) larvae, which can pass into the milk and be ingested by the foal. Roundworms can rob the foal of his full nutritional load, and can *underlie* (be a root cause of) foal diarrhea. This deworming regimen also minimizes overall parasite exposure in the foal; the dewormer transfers to your mare's milk so her foal will also receive its benefits.

(photo by Zita)

CHAPTER TEN

POTENTIAL
PREGNANCY PROBLEMS

**A colorful Appaloosa colt, his resplendent blanket a fine example of
the breed.** (photo by Cappy Jackson)

COLIC CRISIS

I breed Arabian Horses for halter; performance is my secondary goal. My Arabian Horse mare, Krucicca ("Cici"), was 314 days in foal when she bloated with colic. My trainer, Mark Jamieson, and his team worked all day to walk her. My veterinarian was out three times that day to check on her condition and provide medication. In the late afternoon, they decided to move her to the Georgia Veterinary School hospital in Athens.

At 7:00 P.M., a hospital veterinarian called and told me they were taking a "wait and see" attitude with Cici. At 11:00 P.M., the veterinary team decided that Cici needed surgery; the surgery lasted for three hours. No obstructions were found. They relieved the bloat and sewed my mare back up, giving her baby about a 50/50 chance of survival.

At 7:00 the next morning, a hospital veterinarian called and told me that Cici was doing well. By 10:00 A.M., I received another telephone call telling me that Cici had bloated again and was going back into surgery. This time, they found a calcified piece of lead rope in her intestines and removed it. But now, they gave her baby a less than 2 percent chance of survival. In fact, one veterinarian told me the fetus was dead, and they wanted to keep Cici in the hospital until she aborted it.

I was devastated! This was my first foal in nearly twenty years, my mare was in foal to the number-one stallion in the country, and I was being told there was no hope that the fetus would survive.

Cici stayed at the veterinary hospital for almost a week. The veterinary team performed ultrasound scans every two days to check on the fetus. Then, a miracle occurred. At the end of the week, the team found that the fetus was still very much alive and doing well! They then sent Cici back to my trainer's barn.

After all that trauma, Cici delivered a healthy foal. At the time of this writing, Afire Fighter is a healthy stallion in training for his National Futurity as a pending three-year-old! And Cici is in foal to U.S. National Top Ten Western horse Michal T Mahogany.

—Jill A. Zamowski, Druid Oak Arabians, McCalla, Alabama

IN A PERFECT WORLD, YOUR MARE WILL HAVE A PROBLEM-FREE pregnancy. Most pregnancy problems can be avoided with careful mare care. If you follow our broodmare-care advice in chapter 9, you'll preempt most problems. But the reality is, they sometimes do happen, despite your best efforts. When something goes awry, will you know when to call for help? What should you do if your soon-to-deliver mare shows signs of colic but still wants to eat? What should you do if your mare has far passed her due date?

Here, Heidi Immegart, DVM, MS, PhD, will help you identify and avoid ten potential threats to your mare's health and pregnancy. Dr. Immegart is a breeding specialist and regularly presents information at The Ohio State University's veterinarian-training workshops. She'll teach you what early trouble signs to look for, and tell you what you need to do to keep your mare healthy and the baby growing strong.

Note: If you're concerned about *anything* regarding your pregnant mare, don't hesitate to call your veterinarian.

Potential problem #1: Spontaneous abortion.

Mares may spontaneously abort pregnancies (that is, prematurely end gestation without human intervention) for many reasons. When a fetus becomes ill or dies in utero, the mare aborts it so that she can breed again. In the wild, such rebreeding helps to ensure herd survival. Other pregnancy problems can also result in an abortion. Here, we'll explain two common illnesses that cause abortion—*EHV-1* (equine herpesvirus-1, subtype 1; a subtype of equine viral rhinopneumonitis also known as "viral herpes abortion") and *EHV-4* (equine herpesvirus-4, a subtype of equine viral rhinopneumonitis also known as the "respiratory rhino virus"). We'll also go over another cause of abortion—infection that develops because of poor vulva conformation.

Herpesvirus

Timeline: A mare may contract herpes at any point during gestation. The viruses are easily spread to a mare's respiratory tract through the air and via direct contact with other horses. They can also be carried on caretakers' clothing, and lie dormant in hair, on animals, and in the environment. The viruses can survive for up to forty-two days when attached to "friendly" materials.

(photo by Cappy Jackson)

Without proper vaccination, horses may easily spread the disease within a herd, causing an *abortion storm* among broodmares. An abortion storm occurs when many mares within a herd abort fetuses and infect one another. Herpesvirus abortions occur after the seven month of pregnancy.

Early warning signs: While some horses with herpes show signs of discomfort and respiratory problems, others show no signs at all. A mare with a healthy immune system may fend off the virus without appearing ill. Still, the virus lives on in her vascular system; her white blood cells infect the fetus. The abortion itself may be your only clue to know your mare was infected.

"It's such a nasty virus," Dr. Immegart says. "If your mare is exposed thirty days into a pregnancy, you may not see signs in your mare, but the disease harbors in the fetus. It can cause an abortion much later in gestation. Your mare may look fine, then abort later in the day."

Some mares do show signs that an abortion is imminent. Herpes-infected mares may prematurely develop *mammary glands* (secretion-producing organs responsible for milk production).

What's happening: Herpes viruses travel through the mare's system and into the fetus. Abortion occurs with rapid separation of the placenta, which causes fetal suffocation. Near-term fetuses may be born alive.

Is it serious? Of course, it may be lethal for the fetus. Some foals are born weak and survive. However, your infected mare should be able to conceive and give birth to healthy foals after a herpesvirus abortion. She may carry the herpes virus for life, and, if she's not vaccinated, may experience viral spread again. A regular vaccination schedule will diminish the likelihood of abortion occurrence.

What you should do: "It's important to make sure your mare follows an appropriate vaccination schedule before conceiving," Dr. Immegart says. "Vaccinate your horses whether or not they have contact with other horses, because of other means of disease transmission." A live-vaccine immunity lasts up to six months, but can only be given to open mares. If you vaccinate immediately before breeding your mare, you need not administer another vaccine until midpregnancy. If your mare is already pregnant, ask your veterinarian to supply a killed vaccine. The live vaccine may be active enough to infect a growing fetus and cause an abortion; the killed vaccine won't prevent further outbreaks. Administer the killed vaccine every other month.

Poor Vulvar Conformation

Timeline: Your mare's *vulva* (external female genitalia) protects her reproductive system from outside contaminants. It should be airtight and vertical, with the top at the brim of her pelvis.

"If the vulva is tipped severely, or above the brim of the pelvis, you risk air coming in," Dr. Immegart warns. "The abdominal cavity has negative pressure, so any time that the vulva opens up, air, dirt, and bacteria get sucked into the uterus and edges close to the fetus.

"If the placenta becomes contaminated, it can cause fetal loss and abortion late term—it can even cause babies to be weak at birth. The baby may have been sick during the end of gestation."

Early warning signs: It's best to have your mare's genitalia evaluated, thereby warning you of the risk before you breed. As with abortions caused by herpes viruses, you may not see any warning signs to let you know a pregnancy will end. (See chapter 2.) However, you might see final mammary-gland development, which is caused by fetal stress.

If you suspect your mare has herpes and you see her mammary glands develop long before her due date, call your veterinarian immediately. He or she may be able to administer hormones to help your mare maintain pregnancy.

"This is one of the few times I'll use hormone therapy," Dr. Immegart says. "You may be able to maintain the pregnancy long enough to develop a viable foal. The drawback? It may or may not work. If the foal lives, he may be weak or sick at birth."

What's happening: A virus can infect the placenta, which stops providing the fetus with crucial *progesterone* (the hormone necessary to maintain pregnancy). Without proper nutrition, the growing fetus can't survive. The mare may begin to show signs associated with impending delivery—developing mammary glands and showing abdominal discomfort. The mare's body begins contractions to expel the sick placenta and the deceased fetus.

"Once bacteria invade the uterus, they can infect the placenta—a great environment for them to thrive," says Dr. Immegart. "Since the placenta is important for the fetus's growth and oxygen supply, it has to be healthy. When it's invaded by bacteria, that area becomes nonfunctional. A smaller and smaller placental area tries to support a larger and larger fetus. It can't work that way. The pregnancy ends."

Is it serious? Yes. Poor vulvar conformation may keep your mare from becoming pregnant or cause her to lose pregnancies.

What you should do: Ask your veterinarian to check your mare's vulvar conformation before breeding season each year. As mares age, vulvar conformation may change. If there's a problem, the structure can be corrected with *Caslick's surgery* (a procedure in which your veterinarian will stitch your mare's vulva; see chapter 6).

If your mare aborts the fetus, have her evaluated by your veterinarian as soon as possible. Ask him or her to perform a culture and biopsy at least two weeks post-delivery to check for infection and uterine status.

Also, find and save the aborted material for your veterinarian to examine. "It may sound morbid, but it may help your veterinarian understand what happened and possibly help prevent abortions in the future," notes Dr. Immegart. "In a quick exam, I may see evidence of whether your mare had herpes, or placentitis from poor vulva conformation."

Potential problem #2: Colic.

If your pregnant mare has a history of colic, watch her carefully. If your mare has had colic surgery in the past, watch even more closely.

Timeline: Horses can colic at any time. Pregnant mares aren't more likely to colic than other horses, but the risks are higher when mare and fetus are involved.

Early warning signs: Make sure your mare eats regularly, drinks, and passes manure regularly. What goes in should pass through in a timely fashion. If your mare kicks at her belly or attempts to bite at her barrel, keep watch, and

(photo by Cappy Jackson)

call your veterinarian. While these signs can be confused with normal pregnancy discomfort at the end of gestation, they may also be signs of colic. Cribbing increases the likelihood of recurrent colic.

What's happening: Your mare's digestive tract may be upset because of feeding changes or because she's swallowed excess gas during cribbing episodes. Your mare may kick at her belly and even roll to get relief. As she rolls, she may twist her already-agitated bowels. A twist will shock her system and stress the fetus.

Is it serious? Yes. Colic in pregnant mares can lead to *endotoxemia* (toxins released into the bloodstream, causing hemorrhages, kidney failure, and shock). If your mare's bowel twists and she needs to have colic surgery while she's pregnant, you'll risk the pregnancy—and your mare's life.

If your mare has colicked in the past and required surgery, pregnancy may be difficult. Horses' intricate bowels may form adhesions after surgery.

"Think twice about breeding a mare that has had colic surgery in the past and has extensive adhesions," Dr. Immegart warns. "Colic surgery

HOW TO TAKE VITAL SIGNS

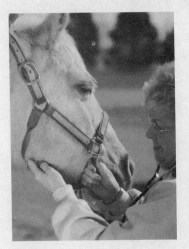

At Swalde Quarter Horses, Marilyn Swalde checks her mare's pulse. (photo by Heidi Nyland)

Knowing your mare's healthy vital signs will help you chart what's normal for her, as well as alert you to potential problems. When you notice that your mare is uncomfortable and you see major differences in her temperature, respiration, pulse, gut sounds, or gum color, it's time to call your veterinarian. Have vital-sign data on hand during the phone call to help your veterinarian know how serious the problem is. Here's a list of typical vital signs and how to check your mare.

Temperature: Normal temperature for a horse is 99.5 to 100.5 degrees Fahrenheit. Fevers, disease, and overheating your early pregnant mare can cause her to lose the pregnancy. Check her temperature rectally with a digital thermometer for speed and precision. Slide the thermometer in against the side of her rectal wall so that you miss fecal balls.

Respiration: Your mare's respiration should be slow. If she has an upper respiratory disease, she may breathe more quickly. High respiratory rates aren't often linked with pregnancy, but if your mare is sick, her respiration may be quick. Simply listen to your horse breathe and note any straining.

Pulse: Average pulse for a horse is between thirty and thirty-six beats per minute. Pulse rates can increase during gestation as your mare's blood volume increases. It may increase to forty or a little above. If you're getting pulse rates of sixty beats per minute or more, something painful is happening. An increased pulse is often an indication of pain.

Check your mare's pulse with a stethoscope. Place the stethoscope on your mare's heart, which is on her chest, tucked behind her left elbow.

If you don't have a stethoscope, place your fingertips under your mare's jaw line. You'll find an artery as wide as a pencil. It runs obliquely across the bottom front of her jaw. To feel it, place your fingers lightly under her jaw and roll them back and forth; you'll feel something roll like a straw. You'll also feel a pulse. Count beats per minute, just as you would when listening to your mare's heartbeat.

Gut sounds: The fetus will take up a significant portion of your mare's abdomen. While you usually want to hear gut sounds to ensure all is moving along, you may not hear as much from your pregnant mare. The baby may be in the way. To listen for gut sounds, place a stethoscope along your mare's barrel and flank area. Listen carefully in several places.

Gum color: A horse's gums should be soft pink. Whitish gums can indicate pain or blood loss. Any angry-looking color (such as purple or dark red) indicates shock or toxemia. To check, gently lift your mare's upper lip and look at her gums.

Checking the mare's gut sounds.
(photo by Heidi Nyland)

doesn't mean you can't breed your mare, but you may want to know how much scar tissue there is."

What you should do: Take any measure possible to prevent cribbing and intense colic episodes. Cutting out her wind-sucking habit with a specially designed collar will help avoid colic. If your mare appears uncomfortable and refuses feed, call your veterinarian. While you wait for the doctor, walk your mare or tie her to prevent her from rolling.

Potential Problem #3: Fescue toxicosis.

Fescue grass is a ground-cover favorite. Its wide, flat leaves, drought resistance, and adaptability to most any soil allow it to easily cover large lawns and pastures. The grass covers an estimated 35 million acres in the United States. However, tall fescue is susceptible to fungus and isn't appropriate for mares during their first and last thirty days of pregnancy. The fungus, an ergot alkaloid-producing endophyte called *Acremonium coenophialum,* can cause mares to abort or hold pregnancies too long.

Timeline: If a mare is fed infected fescue grass or hay during her first trimester, she may abort her pregnancy or have trouble conceiving. In the last thirty days, a mare on infected fescue will hold her fetus, potentially making pregnancy last up to thirteen months, instead of the usual eleven months, eleven days. In that time, the fetus continues to grow.

Early warning signs: If your mare doesn't conceive at the start of breeding season, have your hay and pastures checked for infected fescue. If your pregnant mare is progressing well, keep an eye out for her developing mammary gland. She should develop a mammary gland before or during month 11. If the gland isn't developing, she may be holding onto the pregnancy.

What's happening: The fungus that thrives on fescue is toxic to your mare. Once in her bloodstream, the ergot alkaloid affects the mare a number of ways. If the presence is prolonged, the fetus can overgrow during the time frame. *Prolactin* (the hormone that initiates milk production) diminishes, mammary glands develop, and the placenta is sickened, thereby affecting fetal development.

Is it serious? Yes. "If your mare eats too much infected grass, you'll end up with an overdue foal with a thick placenta," Dr. Immegart warns. "She'll 'red bag.' That is, instead of breaking water, she'll try to deliver the whole placenta intact—it's like trying to push a water balloon through a keyhole. When that happens, babies suffocate easily. Plus, the baby may be too big to fit through the pelvis. If you don't act quickly, there's going to be a problem."

A mare that consumes large quantities of infested fescue can suffer from prolonged gestation, abortion, premature separation of the *chorioallantois* (a membrane that joins the placenta to the uterus), *dystocia* (difficult birth), a thickened placenta, and a retained placenta. She also might not have enough milk for her foal.

The fetus will be in trouble if it stays in utero too long and continues to grow. Foals born after a long gestation may have large frames, poorly developed muscles, overgrown hooves, and faulty coordination.

If your mare suffered from fescue toxicosis once, she may be fine during the next breeding season as long as she's not on fescue and barring injuries from foaling problems.

What you should do: If you're not sure of what type of grass you have in your pastures, contact your local county extension office. If you have fescue, have it tested to see if the problem-causing organism is present. For about thirty dollars, Auburn University's Fescue Diagnostic Center accepts test samples. For information on sending samples of grass and seeds for testing, write the center at: 209 Life Science Building, Auburn Univer-

Weed-free alfalfa hay provides plenty of protein for the mother-to-be.
(photo by Heidi Nyland)

sity, AL 36849; or visit www.ag.auburn.edu/dept/entplp/services/fescue.htm.

Once you know about your pasture, do your best to manage your mare's time on the grass. Ideally, you'll avoid fescue altogether. If that's not an option, make sure your mare is away from the fescue source during her first and final months.

If your mare has eaten fescue-infected hay and is overdue, call your veterinarian. When your mare is ready to deliver, watch her closely—and be prepared. You'll need to cut through the thick placenta—the "red bag" described earlier. (For more on delivery problems and how to assist your mare, see chapter 12.)

"This is the one thing I prepare clients for, and let them know they need to be bold and brave if I'm not there," Dr. Immegart says. "If you see something that looks like red velvet coming from the back of your mare, cut it first, then call your vet."

RARE PROBLEMS

Mammary-gland problems: Your mare's mammary gland helps her produce *colostrum* (first milk) and subsequent milk for her newborn foal. In rare cases, your mare may not develop the gland, so you'll need to find an alternative source of colostrum and milk.

Your mare might also have the opposite problem: She might start streaming milk before she delivers. While a little bit of milk on her teats is normal, streaming quantities of milk is not. Have a backup of colostrum on hand in case she's dripped away the vital nutrients.

Umbilical cord constrictions: It's possible for your fetus's umbilical cord to wrap around a leg and effectively amputate it. A fetus can also spin and cut off its own blood supply. This will usually cause an abortion, or in rare cases, birth defects. Such constrictions are more common in Miniature Horses and other small breeds than in full-sized horses. A Mini's different abdominal proportions may allow the growing baby to spin and twist its umbilical cord.

Potential problem #4: Internal injury.

If you have more than one broodmare, or your pregnant mare is pastured with others, you've seen the herd compete for position. They may routinely kick at one another. Horses are also susceptible to other strange accidents that can send their bodies into shock—running through fences, finding that one pesky nail sticking up along a run-in shed, falling during trail rides. While these types of accidents rarely impact growing fetuses, a pregnant mare can easily sustain internal injuries if contaminants are forced into her body.

"Don't house your mares with geldings that still have breeding instincts," Dr. Immegart says. "Geldings can penetrate your mare, and you don't want anything dirty inside a pregnant mare. In the wild, new harem stallions may rape mares and rebreed them with their genetics."

Timeline: Your mare can sustain an injury at any time during gestation. If your mare is close to full-term, a fall or a kick from another horse may have more impact on the fetus than it would earlier in the pregnancy, because there's less protective fluid surrounding the fetus.

Early warning signs: Keep an eye on your mare to make sure she's not being hurt by other mares or geldings in her pasture.

What's happening: The growing fetus is well-protected from the outside, but internal contamination and shock affect the fetus as much as your mare. If your mare is hurt and stressed, her baby will also be stressed.

Is it serious? It depends on what happened to what body part. Horses are resilient, and can manage most kicks, cuts, and falls. "I've never known of a case where a kick resulted in abortion," Dr. Immegart says. "I've seen mares get whaled on and still maintain pregnancy if they're watched closely afterward. Then again, you don't know what you're going to get."

What you should do: Carefully choose your pregnant mare's pasture buddies. Make sure any geldings she's housed with will leave her alone. Likewise, make sure that other mares aren't too aggressive. While a kick isn't usually life-threatening for mom or baby, you don't want your pregnant mare to be chased and bullied. Stress can cause more problems than visible injuries.

When your mare is close to term, consider moving her to a level pen where she can relax without threats from other horses. Also, when exercising her in the last month, minimize rapid changes in direction and speed that might lead to a fall. As the fetus grows, your mare's balance might be off. She might slip and fall to catch her balance. A severe fall can cause pregnancy problems.

This mare has a roomy foaling stall, deeply bedded with straw.
(photo by Heidi Nyland)

NO PROBLEM!

Many new horse breeders are alarmed when their horse shows any signs of discomfort. Don't worry; some "symptoms" are perfectly normal.

Abdominal discomfort: Your mare will show signs of abdominal discomfort as the fetus repositions itself immediately before delivery. Your mare might lie down and get up quickly, look at her belly, and show typical colic signs. She'll look restless, but she'll want to eat—that's how you'll know your mare is uncomfortable, but not colicky.

Edema: *Edema* is fluid accumulation in the tissues on the underside of your mare's belly. "It's like women's ankles swelling when they're pregnant," Dr. Immegart says. "There's compression on the vessels that drain the mare's back end because of the pregnancy." You might see your mare's sides stick out in seemingly odd shapes. Point out the edema to your veterinarian when he or she visits, as a precaution. However, in most cases, the swelling is nothing to worry about and will go down on its own.

Heat: Although you might think that your mare coming into heat is a sign she's not pregnant, it's actually quite common for pregnant mares to look like they're in heat. Estrogen buildup in their bodies causes them to show signs of heat. "I once had a tease mare that showed heat throughout her pregnancies," Immegart says. "She worked as a tease mare until the day she delivered. She would squat and urinate as soon as the stud was there."

If your mare is hurt, call your veterinarian. Ask him or her which medications are safe for mare and baby. "You don't want to use certain tranquilizers and some other drugs during pregnancy," Dr. Immegart says. "But if the mare's injury is life-threatening, you may have to risk the fetus's health to save your mare."

Potential problem #5: Equine protozoal myeloencephalitis.

Equine protozoal myeloencephalitis (EPM) can settle into your mare's system if she eats feed contaminated by the protozoan *Sarcocystis falcatula*. This parasite can attach to your mare's neurological system, causing weight loss, coordination problems, and even paralysis.

Timeline: Mares with managed EPM can produce healthy foals. However, the symptoms may worsen at any time. Stress can bring on symptoms at any time during pregnancy or delivery. Your healthy mare can contract EPM at any time during her pregnancy.

Early warning signs: EPM presents different symptoms in different horses. Watch for sudden stumbles, unexplained weight loss, and lameness. "It depends on where the protozoan migrates," Dr. Immegart says. "Some mares may move normally, but can't keep on weight, while others walk with difficulty. It depends on which area of the central nervous system is affected—and you won't see specific progressive signs at a certain time."

What's happening: EPM manifests in horses after traveling first through other host animals. The parasite first reproduces and spreads through birds, then small mammals, such as opossums, raccoons, and armadillos. Although these small mammals don't get sick, they further spread the protozoan through excrement that ends up on hay and grass. Your mare eats the forage, and becomes infected.

Is it serious? Yes. "Worst-case scenario, you could lose your mare," Dr. Immegart warns. "One mare with EPM conceived, then stress brought on more symptoms. Her back end would twist forward. She died suddenly during gestation."

But having EPM doesn't necessarily mean a tragic end. "Another mare in the same herd contracted the parasite while she was pregnant," Dr. Immegart continues. "She was treated immediately during that first gestation, delivered a seemingly healthy foal, and delivered two more foals in later years. She hasn't had any trouble with her pregnancies. Some mares do fine, but know the risks."

What you should do: If you notice EPM symptoms, contact your veterinarian immediately. New medications can improve your mare's chance of stopping the protozoan's progress.

Potential problem # 6: Laminitis.

Simply put, *laminitis* is a painful disease affecting horses' hooves. Horses feel pain when *laminae* (membrane layers in the foot that secure the coffin bone—the largest bone in a horse's foot—to the hoof wall) are inflamed. The disease, often called founder, can be caused by overfeeding, colic, high fever, and when toxins are released into the horse's bloodstream. The term *founder* implies chronic laminitis. Horses that have foundered have rotated coffin bones, often as a result of inflamed laminae.

Mares that have struggled with laminitis in the past may be more susceptible to problems when they are pregnant. Even mares that have never had a problem before can founder if the placenta is retained after delivery.

Timeline: Laminitis attacks can happen at any time. Be especially watchful after your foal's birth to make sure the placenta passes easily. A retained placenta can cause laminitis after delivery. (See below.)

Early warning signs: Watch your mare for signs of lameness. Also, check her feet for heat and an increased digital pulse.

What's happening: If your mare retains the placenta after foal delivery, toxins may enter her bloodstream and impact her feet. When blood flow to your horse's laminae is disrupted, or when toxins are introduced to the bloodstream, the sensitive structures weaken and reduce their grip on the hoof wall. In extreme cases, the laminae separate from the hoof wall and the coffin bone begins to rotate.

Is it serious? Possibly. "Maintaining a foundered mare just means being on top of things so that you aren't fighting the battle at the end," Dr. Immegart says. "She can be just fine throughout her pregnancy."

What you should do: If your pregnant mare has foundered in the past, check her daily. Make sure she's standing correctly, and place your hand on her feet to check for heat. Work with your veterinarian to place your laminitic mare on a diet rich in forage, but lacking energy-pumping grains. (Excess carbohydrates can lead to inflamed laminae.) Keep her hooves well trimmed. Make sure all feed cans have locking lids so your mare can't help herself to extra snacks.

If you treat your laminitic mare with the nonsteroidal anti-inflammatory phenylbutazone ("bute"), make sure to take her off of the drug before the end of gestation. Banamine is a safe substitution. Bute can close the hole in the fetus's heart before delivery. This hole is natural in utero so the fetus can get oxygen from its dam. "Foals in utero don't get oxygen through their lungs, they get it from the placenta," Dr. Immegart explains. "Oxygenated blood circulates through the hole in their heart to vital fetal tissues. If that hole closes too soon, the fetus won't have oxygen."

(photo by Cappy Jackson)

After birth, your mare should pass the placenta within three hours. If you're worried about her laminitis, or if she doesn't deliver the placenta in a timely fashion, ask your veterinarian to administer *oxytocin* (a hormone that stimulates smooth muscle contraction of the uterus). "If a mare has foundered in the past, I'll have people giving them oxytocin soon after the delivery so that they don't retain the placenta," Dr. Immegart notes.

Potential problem #7: Malnutrition.

Proper broodmare nutrition is an important component needed to sustain pregnancies and produce healthy foals. (See chapter 9.) Most caring horse owners overfeed instead of underfeed their horses. Still, even caring horse owners have been known to unknowingly reduce their mares' feed, believing the mares were just gaining weight.

"One owner I worked with thought his mare was getting fat and cut back her feed," Dr. Immegart recalls. "They'd just purchased the mare and didn't know she was pregnant. They saw her gaining weight and thought they were doing the right thing."

Timeline: The mare's nutrition may affect the fetus at every stage. If the mare isn't receiving nutrients, her body will do everything possible to provide proper nutrition to the developing fetus.

Early warning signs: If your mare has a round belly and a sunken spine, she may be pregnant instead of overweight.

What's happening: Without enough nutrients, a mare will begin to use stored fat for needed energy. Her body searches for nutrients wherever possible. If few nutrients are available, she'll suffer malnutrition, and her fetus may miss out on nutrients crucial for healthy growth. Also, a malnourished mare may change posture. As she does, her vulva conformation also changes, allowing air and infection-causing bacteria to infiltrate the womb. A malnourished mare might abort, or deliver weak and sickly foals.

Is it serious? Yes. Malnutrition can cause developmental problems and lead to death of the mare and baby. "I've seen extremely malnourished mares that have not lost their babies," Dr. Immegart says. "One mare came into the country with severe malnutrition. She maintained her pregnancy, but the baby was born weak and with a cleft palate. He didn't make it. The mare had gained weight before she delivered and she delivered fine. The reason for the foal's cleft palate was unknown."

What you should do: If you're having trouble keeping weight on a mare, consult your veterinarian to discuss feeding strategies. Your vet may also test your mare for EPM and other diseases that can present "skinny" symptoms. If you purchase a pregnant mare that appears malnourished, have her examined as soon as possible. Providing a nutrient-filled diet will help her baby grow optimally.

Potential problem #8: Obesity.

An overweight horse isn't pleasantly plump. Obesity can lead to laminitis. And, in pregnant mares, pelvic fat pads may result in less room for baby to come out. You're not doing your mare any favors by feeding her extra portions.

"Many people have mares that gain weight at the start of pregnancy," Dr. Immegart says. "They think that their pregnant mare needs more feed immediately after conception. It's not true. Half of fetal weight is gained in the last trimester. At the end of the second trimester, the fetus weighs about forty pounds. Compared to a thousand-pound horse, that's not a lot of foal to feed.

"Mares usually need an extra boost during the last trimester," she continues. "But during the first two trimesters, you usually don't need to do anything extra, unless they're lactating."

Timeline: Monitor your horse's weight throughout gestation.

Early warning signs: As your mare gains excessive weight, you'll first see fat pockets develop on her shoulders, neck, and rump. If fat pads surround her rump, she may already be heading for trouble.

What's happening: As fat builds up, it deposits around the *pelvic canal*—the space the foal must pass through for delivery. The foal's shoulders are the widest part, so limiting the space it has to pass through can cause trouble for mare and foal.

Is it serious? Not unless you let your mare's weight get out of hand. Weight can be managed at any point during gestation. You don't want an excessively over- or underweight mare. If you don't monitor your mare's weight, she may have difficulty at delivery.

What you should do: Don't feed for two as soon as your mare conceives. Keep her feed portions fairly even throughout early pregnancy. (See chapter 9.) As gestation progresses, check your mare's body condition regularly.

Potential problem #9: Twinning.

Twin fetuses almost never develop to be healthy, live foals. Most often, one twin receives most of the nutrients and more space than the other one. If twins live, one is usually smaller than the other. Oftentimes, neither twin is totally healthy.

Timeline: Ask your veterinarian to keep an eye out for twins—and triplets—as early as 14 to 15 days into the pregnancy. By Day 25, there's little you can do to limit the pregnancy without risking all embryos involved. (See chapter 9.)

Early warning signs: If a mare has produced twins in the past, she'll most likely produce multiple eggs and embryos again. While there are no external signs to signify twins, your mare's breed may determine the likelihood that she will begin growing two foals. On average, 25 to 35 percent of Thoroughbred mares ovulate multiple eggs, while Quarter Horses ovulate multiple eggs 15 to 20 percent of the time.

What's happening: After the mare ovulates multiple eggs to be fertilized (or in rare cases, when one egg divides), two embryos begin competing for uterus space. Often, mares resolve one pregnancy without outside help. If both embryos survive, usually one has more space to grow than the other; the one with less space may die in utero. Because the uterus is a sterile envi-

Ultrasound is an invaluable tool for breeders. (photo by Heidi Nyland)

ronment, the second embryo remains in the womb and is delivered soon after the live foal. If both fetuses survive and grow equally for some time, delivery can be a problem. Multiple foals may compete for space through the birth canal.

Is it serious? It can be. Multiple foals are threatened because neither may receive enough oxygen and nutrition. If both foals live long enough to grow fairly large, they'll compete for space and nutrients. At birth, the mare and foals may be at risk when too many limbs compete for delivery room. Your mare might become injured if both foals simultaneously present one leg through the birth canal.

"I once worked with a Thoroughbred mare that had a triplet pregnancy," Dr. Immegart says. "When I first examined her, I saw all three embryos, but I thought one or more may be a cyst. I told the owner I wanted to see the mare within five days. In that time, I'd be able to tell if all three were growing, or if one or more were cysts so didn't grow. The owner didn't give me access to the mare until the mare was two months pregnant. At that point, one embryo had died and the mare still had a twin pregnancy. The owner didn't want to abort at sixty days, so she let the pregnancy go. The mare aborted at nine months and she had a retained placenta. One of the placentas stayed attached too long. The owner ended up with no babies and a sick mare."

What you should do: Work with your veterinarian to schedule regular pregnancy checks that include ultrasound scans. (See chapter 9.) Catching a multiple-embryo pregnancy early on will allow you options and increase your chances of having at least one healthy foal. Your vet can manually limit the pregnancy, or give your mare hormones so that she'll abort and you can rebreed.

Potential problem # 10: Uterine artery ruptures.

Aging mares are at heightened risk for uterine artery ruptures—literally bursting the artery that supplies blood from the mare to the fetus during gestation.

Timeline: Aged mares are at risk during gestation and delivery. Mares aged sixteen and over are at risk. When mares reach eighteen, their risk increases again. Mares in their twenties are at high risk.

Early warning signs: There's little warning that the artery has ruptured. You may see your mare look disoriented or uncomfortable at the onset of a bleed into the *broad ligament* (the large ligament that supports the uterus). You may also hear a chilling cry during the rupture.

"I've heard two mares die during bleed outs," Dr. Immegart says. "It's the most eerie whinny I've ever heard. They seem to know that something serious is happening. They may feel faint and disoriented. It's chilling. They lost control, then crashed to the ground. It's an awful way to see a horse die—especially if the mare has been a friend. It happens abruptly, acutely, and there's no way to stop it."

What's happening: The uterine artery is a large artery that supplies the pregnancy. Because the elasticity is lost with age, it can rupture when it's under great stress. The artery may bleed into the broad ligament, where it can be confined. If it ruptures into the abdomen, it starts an uncontrolled bleed out and the mare will die.

Is it serious? Yes, uterine artery ruptures are often fatal. If your mare survives, she shouldn't be bred in the future. The artery will almost always rupture again.

What you should do: If you choose to breed an older mare, watch her closely—especially during and after delivery. "If you're present, you may be able to save the foal, but oftentimes, the mare won't make it," Dr. Immegart warns. "If you have a mare whose only purpose in life is to produce babies, breed her. If she's a pet or a beloved family member, think twice. It's an awful way to watch her die."

If your aged mare shows unusual behavior and uncomfortable signs after delivery, tie her so that she can't lie down. If a bleed begins and drains into the broad ligament, you may be able to confine the blood by keeping her still. If she lies down, then gets up, rolls, etc., she'll likely allow the blood to flow out of the broad ligament and into her abdomen—a fatal move.

(photo by Cappy Jackson)

CHAPTER ELEVEN

THE FOALING
ENVIRONMENT

This beautiful colt became a national champion and distinguished sire: Thee Desperado, owned by Arabians Ltd., Waco, Texas. (photo by Randi Clark)

163

BEST-LAID PLANS

Our family breeds Arabian Horses for show and recreation, but we never kept broodmares onsite. That all changed when we rescued a mare that had been bred three days before we got her. She was very thin and had had no real care. We brought her home and had her checked thirty days later. She was in foal.

We gave our new mare everything she could ever want and need while she was pregnant, learning along the way. We didn't have proper foaling facilities, so we found a place close to both our house and our veterinarian's clinic. We planned to take our mare to the facility when she was ten months pregnant.

Unfortunately, that didn't happen. When our mare was a little over nine and a half months pregnant, a neighbor came to our door and said he thought that "the horse in the front pasture is dying." We ran out to our pasture and found the baby was almost completely out of the mare, delivered six weeks early.

Our premature foal—a filly—was weak, but she was alive. We called our veterinarian immediately, who advised us to hand-feed the filly for the first twenty-four hours; the filly couldn't nurse because she wasn't able to stand. We also had to stay with the foal 24/7 for the first three days.

The good news: At this writing, our filly is two years old—and she's as strong and healthy as an ox!

—Martha Smith, Escondido, California

YOUR MARE AND HER UNBORN FOAL APPEAR TO BE HEALTHY and everything is going smoothly. It's time to prepare the foaling environment.

"Actually, the best place for a mare to foal—weather permitting—is in a big, clean, grassy pasture with continuous fencing that comes all the way down to the ground, so the foal can't roll out," says mare-care expert Barb Crabbe, DVM, who runs a foaling station in Oregon City, Oregon.

"But the downside of a pasture is that an unattended birth puts the foal at a high risk for disaster—and it's hard to attend to a foaling in a pasture, unless you follow the mare around 24/7."

In fact, 90 percent of mares foal without intervention from an attendant; 10 percent do require some kind of intervention to ensure the health of the mare and/or foal—most commonly the foal. The catch is that you won't know until foaling time whether intervention will be necessary, and it's that 10 percent chance you *will* need to intervene for which you need to prepare. The best way to do that is to create a confined foaling environment where you can closely monitor your mare.

Here, Dr. Crabbe describes how you can help ensure the healthiest and safest environment for your newborn's entry into the outside world. She covers the advantages and drawbacks of having your mare have her baby in a foaling station versus in a stall in your own barn, then tells how to set up a safe and clean foaling environment.

FOALING-STATION FACTS

Should your mare foal at home or at a foaling station? First, here are some foaling-station pros to keep in mind.

Round-the-clock monitoring.

"It's hugely important that someone be there for the birth of your foal, to take care of any emergencies," says Dr. Crabbe. "If the foal isn't positioned correctly and your mare is unable to deliver without help, the lives of both your mare and her foal are at risk. You'll also need to ensure the foal is normal, up, nursing in time to get the colostrum, passing the meconium [first excrement], etc.

"At a foaling station, a knowledgeable attendant will be there 24/7, either at your mare's side, or watching a video monitor," she continues. "It's hard to do that yourself, and still work and have a life." (For a timeline on the foal's vital statistics the first forty-eight hours of life, see chapter 13.) An attendant can also check your mare's milk for elevated calcium levels—a fairly reliable sign your mare is getting close to foaling time.

Onsite veterinarian.

You'll look for a foaling station with an onsite reproductive veterinarian (or one close by, on call), who can handle any foaling emergency that might come up. "If a mare is ready to foal, we'll sleep at the barn," notes Dr. Crabbe.

Experienced team.

Not only do foaling stations offer round-the-clock monitoring and a veterinarian onsite or on call, but there's usually a whole team of experienced foaling attendants ready to help your mare deliver her foal, and help your foal through the critical first few hours.

Surveillance.

Foaling stations usually have sophisticated surveillance methods—such as foal-ALERT (an electronic predictor sutured to the vulva) or a sweat monitor—to let the attendants know a mare is about to foal. While these can be helpful, Dr. Crabbe advises that you find a place where there's someone actually watching your mare, or at least a video monitor. "I advise having a person there to be safe," she says. "I'm not as comfortable with a device. For example, foal-ALERTs can be set off by strange events—our old one used to go off randomly, which was frustrating. And if the system fails, you can easily miss the foaling."

Of course, if your pregnant mare is off at a foaling station, which might be many miles away from your home, you won't necessarily be there for the birth of the foal. Even if the attendant calls you when your mare's water breaks, you're likely to miss the actual birth, although you can be there for the foal's first precious hours.

A first meeting at Varian Arabians goes like this: Say "hello," then run for your life! (photo by Zita)

If you'd like to witness the birth, but would prefer to keep your mare at a foaling station, ask the manager if you can camp out when the birth looks imminent. "We offer to let the owner sleep at the place," says Dr. Crabbe. "But sometimes, it's hard to know just when the mare is going to foal."

SELECTING A FOALING STATION

Another downside of foaling stations is that the care of your mare and foal are out of your hands, and into the hands of people you might not know at all, or just met when your mare conceived. To alleviate your anxiety, and ensure optimal care for your mare and foal, select the foaling station carefully. Here are some questions to ask as you scout around.

How closely and at what stage will your mare be monitored?

As mentioned, a live attendant, aided by a video monitor, is more reliable than other monitoring methods. "When the time is close," adds Dr. Crabbe, "you want someone watching your mare 24/7—not just checking on her every two hours. Anything can happen in those two hours—you can even lose your foal during a complicated foaling."

At what stage will your mare first be monitored?

Foaling attendants should monitor your mare 24/7 when foaling appears imminent—and even spend the night. (For signs of foaling, see chapter 12.) "We feel like we're doing great if we spend two nights in the barn before the actual foaling event," says Dr. Crabbe.

Is a reliable veterinarian on call?

Of course, you want the veterinarian to be as close as possible to your about-to-foal mare. "I'd want him or her to be no more than twenty minutes away—and specifically on alert for your mare," says Dr. Crabbe.

How much foaling experience do they have?

Ask how long they've been in business and how many foalings they've presided over. The more the better. "Look for a foaling attendant who's done at least one to two seasons," says Dr. Crabbe. "Although an enthusiastic new attendant is often just as good—or even better—especially if the station has an experienced veterinarian on call."

How many mares do they expect to foal out at the same time your mare is due?

The maximum number of mares a foaling station can safely handle depends on the facility. No more than five per attendant is a general rule of thumb, but it's highly variable. When you visit the facility, see whether the staff seems rushed or harried, or whether it appears well-run—and well-stocked with calm, competent personnel.

Important note:

If something should happen to your mare or foal, it doesn't necessarily mean every effort wasn't made to ensure a smooth delivery, notes Dr. Crabbe.

Even if you find a terrific foaling station with alert monitors and a veterinarian hovering over your mare, a foaling disaster can still strike.

YOUR FOALING STALL

If you decide to have your foal born at home, you'll need to set up a safe, healthy environment for your mare and foal. Here are the particulars.

Stall size/configuration.

Your foaling stall needs to be 12-by-24 feet or larger to give your mare enough room to turn and roll as she goes into labor—then lie down and give birth without accidentally crushing her foal against the wall. Larger is fine—and recommended if you have a large mare, such as a big-boned warmblood. The stall should have solid walls *at least* three feet high and that go all the way to the ground so the foal can't roll out or catch a leg.

Tip: Create a 12-by-24-foot stall with a removable wall that gives you two 12-by-12-foot stalls. You'll then have two doors, in case your mare blocks one when she lies down during labor.

Stall doors.

Sliding stall doors are best. They're easy to open, and you can open them partway to sneak a look at your mare—or even sneak into the stall—without disturbing her (and later mare and foal). Double-doors are best, in case your mare goes down in front of one to foal.

Feeder.

Feed your mare off the ground in a feeder with no sharp edges. If you feed her grain, place it in a rubber feed tub that you can easily remove.

Waterer.

Position your mare's water source—either an automatic waterer or water buckets—high, at least four feet off the ground. Use solid brackets with no sharp edges. Your waterer needs to be out of reach of your foal, once he's

There's more growing in the pasture than just green grass: Sacajawea V, bred by Varian Arabians. (photo by Zita)

NEWBORN RUNAWAY

One season, a foal out of an Arabian mare and by a warmblood stallion was born in a stall at the mare owner's home barn. The mare was unattended, and her foal managed to roll right under a small gap at the bottom of the stall door and into the barn aisle. The mare owner is a caring, knowledgeable breeder, but somehow didn't recognize that that small gap might pose a hazard. Plus, the foal arrived two weeks early, taking the owner a bit by surprise.

When the owner went out to feed that morning, her mare was standing in her stall—and the foal was running around the barn. She called me immediately. My biggest concern was that the foal—which obviously hadn't had a chance to nurse—would miss the critical six-hour window in which he needed to absorb the colostrum (antibody-rich first milk). Colostrum helps protect foals from infectious disease and internal parasites until their own antibodies kick in.

My technician—who could get there more quickly than I could—raced out to the mare owner's barn and helped to get mare and foal together. The foal then nursed right away.

Everything else about the foaling—and the foal himself—seemed just fine. I concluded that the foal must've been born earlier that morning, rather than the night before. Tests showed that his blood contained a good supply of antibodies, meaning he *had* gotten his dose of colostrum in time. He was lucky. If he'd missed the window, I probably would've recommended a plasma transfusion. Worse, the little fellow might've gotten a life-threatening infection.

There are two important lessons to be learned from this experience: Monitor your pregnant mare vigilantly, and make sure your foaling-stall walls are solid—*all the way to the ground!*

—*Barb Crabbe, DVM*

---

born. If he drinks water, he won't nurse and will miss out on the proper nutrients in his dam's milk. Foals can also drown in water tanks.

Lighting.

Install indirect light, and keep the light low, so you disturb your mare (and foal, once he's born) as little as possible when you check in. Use a flashlight when necessary rather than turning on harsh overhead lights. You can even use a heat lamp (below) as a light source.

Tip: Prepare to spend time in a darkened stall; most foals are born between 10:00 P.M. and 4:00 A.M., when it's peaceful and quiet.

Heat lamp.

Foals don't regulate their body temperatures well at first, and can die quickly of *hypothermia* (low body temperature caused by exposure to cold). If you live in a cool climate and/or expect your foal to arrive during the cooler months, outfit your foaling stall with a heat lamp. Keep it clean—dust and cobwebs can start a fire. Be sure the cord and plug are in good condition, for safety. Place them out of reach of your foal.

Tip: Note that you don't have to heat the entire stall; your foal will seek warmth if he needs it, and it's best if he can choose between warm and cool areas in the stall, for comfort. Focus the light in the corner nearest the lamp.

Foals need a safe environment and room to test all systems. (photo by Zita)

FOALING RESOURCES

Foal Cams

Saddlebrook BarnCam (920) 474-7776; www.barncams.com

Riverwind Surveillance Supply (888) 409-7665, www.foaling camera.com.

Foaling Monitor

foal-ALERT (800) 237-8861; wwwfoalert.com

Foal cam.

Place a closed-circuit video camera high in a corner of your foaling stall so you'll be able to monitor your mare without interfering with the natural process. Wireless cams are now available. Some suppliers (such as Saddlebrook

One of Varian Arabian's champion-producing broodmares, La Kijan, watching over Kleopatra V. (photo by Zita)

BarnCam) will even host a Web site featuring a live feed of your mare—and then mare and foal. If a foal cam is a little too pricey, a baby monitor (which broadcasts sound only) can be an economical option.

STALL PREP

Before you move your mare into the foaling stall, you'll need to make it safe and clean—then soft and cozy. Here's how.

Do a safety check.

Check for anything that could cause injury to the newborn foal, such as protruding nails and holes, and gaps in the walls. (Keep in mind that the foal might crash land a few times during his first attempts to stand.) Pound down any loose or protruding nails. Nail plywood on any holes large enough to catch a tiny hoof or nose. (This measure will also cut down drafts that might chill your newborn foal.)

Clean and disinfect.

Before you move in your mare, thoroughly clean and disinfect the stall. A clean stall will protect your foal from microorganisms, especially during the first hours when his naval is a crucial potential site of entry. Microorganisms can lead to infection, which in turn can lead to a serious illness—even death. To disinfect the empty stall before move-in, use a phenol-based product, such as Lysol (check the label to be sure) or one containing a quaternary ammonium compound, such as Roccal-D. These disinfectants are best for killing the germs that might threaten your foal. To use, spray or wipe down the stall walls and floor with the product. Before you move in your mare, allow the stall to air-dry. Wait until there are no more fumes, which could harm her lungs.

Tip: You can use a 1:4 Clorox bleach/water mixture to kill germs on cement floors, clean wood, and stall fronts. However, note that organic material—such as manure—inactivates its germ-killing properties.

Bed the stall.

Once your stall is clean, bed your stall with fresh, dry bedding. "We put down rubber mats, then bed with shavings as a base layer for traction, then add fresh, good-quality, non-dusty oat straw," says Dr. Crabbe. "Straw is clean, soft, traditional, and considered ideal for foaling. If you use rubber mats, be sure you completely cover them with shavings, then straw. Otherwise, they can be slippery." You'll need about two big bales of straw for a 12-by-24-foot stall.

Tip: Bank the sides with extra straw to protect your mare in case she lies down against a wall to foal. After she foals, pull the straw onto the stall floor to create a soft bed for baby.

Move in your mare.

Move your mare in the foaling stall approximately thirty days prior to foaling, so she can build up antibodies to any disease-producing contaminants in the

(photo by Zita)

175

environment, whether in the stall or from her barn-mates. These antibodies will be transferred to the colostrum, so her foal will be protected, as well.

Go on poop patrol.

"I pick up poop every time the mare passes it when foaling is impending," says Dr. Crabbe. She also notes that mares sometimes pass a great deal of manure just before foaling—up to ten times her normal volume. Perhaps, Dr. Crabbe suggests, this is nature's way of emptying a mare's GI tract in preparation for the big push.

CHAPTER TWELVE

THE BIRTH

Perhaps the sweetest moment of all, at Paradise Arabians, Dalton, Georgia.
(photo by Randi Clark)

'LITTLE T'

A local horsewoman, Joan Windsor, had a grand old Tennessee Walking Horse broodmare. Her name was Angel, and she was reserved, classy, and absolutely loved being a mom. Joan decided to breed her one last time. Angel was checked in foal with a heartbeat at thirty days, and her pregnancy was uneventful.

When her time came, Joan called, and my wife and I went to assist. By the time we arrived, we could see the colt's head turned back, and we struggled to help him out. Angel was exhausted, and the colt was in bad shape. He'd been deprived of oxygen, so we started mouth-to-mouth. He resuscitated, but barely.

I could see Angel still down, and pushing. I thought she was passing the placenta. But when I looked, there was a lump in it—and the lump was moving! While my wife and Joan worked on the big colt, I turned to his tiny twin, and cleared her face and mouth. She was a little sprite, but tough. She fought for air.

About that time, we decided all three needed "ER"—about three hours away. We loaded Angel and carried her two foals into the trailer. The mare seemed ready to collapse, so I held her up for what seemed like an endless trip, while a friend, Pete Rose, cradled her babies.

The clinic immediately put all three into intensive care. Eventually, they stabilized and came home. Sadly, the big, handsome colt failed again, returned to the center, and was lost despite their heroic efforts.

The little filly wasn't doing much better. Her survival was nip and tuck, as she went back and forth, from home to vet, dragging her IVs with her. She was nothing but attitude. Finally, we decided that she had endured enough poking and prodding. We removed all tubes, and quit all treatment.

Then, an amazing thing happened: The filly started to thrive! She was about as big as a Chihuahua, but she was one tough cookie. Her will to live was utterly ferocious—so we dubbed her "T-Rex." And Angel just loved her to bits.

The filly grew up slightly small for her breed, but sound, strong-bodied, and loving. And now? She's having beautiful babies of her own. But I'll never forget watching "Little T" strut around the pasture with her proud mom. Cute, cute, cute.

—Ken Siefer, Olympic Peninsula, Washington

IT'S FINALLY TIME FOR THE BIG EVENT. AFTER MONTHS OF CARE, your mare is ready to deliver—and you'd like to help *if needed*. While most mares can deliver foals without your intervention, you or an attendant needs to be on hand to help ensure a safe foal delivery. But just what should you check for?

Here, breeding-specialist Heidi Immegart, DVM, MS, PhD, will lead you through the stages you'll witness immediately before, during, and after your foal's birth. After explaining what a "typical" delivery should look like, she'll note the most common birthing difficulties and tell you what action to take. She'll also tell you what supplies to have on hand and when to use them. She'll help you to be prepared, informed, and calm.

"Ninety-five percent of all mares foal without problem," Dr. Immegart says. "If it's happening normally, it'll be over quickly. If you see any problems, call your vet. Do enjoy the experience—it's beautiful."

FOALING SETUP

As your mare's delivery date approaches, make sure you're prepared. Dr. Immegart recommends cleaning up your mare and her foaling stall. Does your mare have a large, clean, well-bedded area where she can foal in peace? Your mare's delivery environment will help ensure she delivers a healthy foal—without the risk of contaminants from dirty bedding or debris. (See chapter 11.)

Dr. Immegart also suggests making sure your foaling kit is well-stocked with supplies that *might* prove handy. "My clients often want to do too much," she says. "Just because you have something ready doesn't mean you need to use it."

The following items will help you prepare for delivery; for a complete listing of items, see "Your Foaling Kit" in chapter 13.

Tail wrap.

Wrapping your mare's tail helps keep her hair—and the contaminants it carries—away from the foal during delivery.

Use a neoprene wrap to cover the top of your mare's tail or a tail bag that will surround all of your mare's tail hair. Use caution if you wrap your mare's tail with tape or fabric. "You don't want to form a tourniquet," Dr. Immegart advises. "I once saw a mare that had her tail wrapped too tightly. The wrap was left on for three weeks. She had to have her tail amputated. Wrap the tail for a short period of time."

Towels.

Gather together four to six large terry towels so that you can help dry off your foal during cold weather. Your mare will lick her baby dry after birth, but if it's below freezing, the licks may not work quickly enough to prevent a chill. Let your mare work first, then assist with a warm towel if the newborn appears chilled.

Foal blanket.

If temperatures fall below freezing, consider outfitting your newly born foal in a blanket. Most blanket suppliers offer foal sizes. But be aware that some mares won't allow you to put a blanket on their foals. "You can try—and it may be worth a try in cold weather—but some mares will rip off a blanket as soon as you put it on," Dr. Immegart warns.

Shortly after giving birth, the mare is on her feet. (photo by Cappy Jackson)

Waxed dental floss.

If the umbilical stump doesn't stop draining blood, floss will help you tie it off with ease (see Stage III, "What to do," for more details on how and when to intervene).

STAGES OF LABOR

Your mare will prepare for delivery, then advance through three stages as she gives birth to a healthy foal. Following is the typical birth procedure. For each stage, you'll learn the signs to watch for, what's happening with the mare, the foal's position, common problems to watch for, and what to do.

Pre-Stage I: Preparation.

What you'll see: In the few weeks, days, and hours before giving birth, your mare will get ready to give birth and care for her newborn foal. You'll see your mare's mammary gland enlarge. Her teats will drop and fill with milk as delivery day approaches. Timing is tricky—some mares may have mammary development six weeks or six hours before delivering.

If you look at your mare from the back, you'll notice that the muscles around her rump are loose when she's ready to deliver. Her body will look more narrow from the back than in days past, due to foal position. If you touch her around her tailhead, you'll feel the loosened ligaments—they'll feel and move like gelatin. The muscles around her vulva will appear soft and flabby.

Want to know when delivery is close? A simple test will tell you when your mare is to deliver within forty-eight hours. "You can test the milk to see if your mare is close," Dr. Immegart says. "Your mare will have an increase in calcium, protein, and *lactose*—milk sugar—and a decrease in salt. You can buy a test kit at your equine-supply store to test your mare's calcium levels. This kit will provide a percentage table to help you gauge how long she has before delivery depending on how much calcium is present. But if you're brave and bold, you can taste the mare's milk to test it. When the taste changes from salty to sweet, delivery should occur within a day or two. It's the crudest test possible, but it's pretty successful."

A solicitous new mother stays close to her newborn, encouraging her to find her feet. (photos by Cappy Jackson)

When your mare is close, you'll also see a waxy substance on the tips of her teats. This waxing occurs when *colostrum* (first milk, rich in vitamins and antibodies) oozes out and settles on the tips.

What's happening: Your mare's body is preparing for birth. She's developing colostrum and milk for her foal. Her body is also reorganizing for delivery. Muscles and ligaments stretch to allow the baby room to move through the birth canal. The foal is repositioning for delivery.

Foal position: The unborn foal must reposition itself immediately before delivery, because your mare carries the fetus crosswise for most of gestation (with the foal's spine perpendicular to hers). "The baby's spine must be in alignment with the mare's spine," Dr. Immegart explains. "When that happens, your mare may suddenly look narrow from the back and deep or low in a side view. If you notice that switch, you should have a foal within three days."

Common problems: Your mare may stream too much colostrum before delivery. If she does, her foal won't have the life-ensuring first meal and passive immunity against diseases he needs. If you see milk flowing from your mare's teats, consider finding another source of colostrum. In rare cases, your mare won't develop a mammary gland or produce milk. (See chapter 10.)

What to do: Collect the items listed in "Foaling Setup." Call your veterinarian to let him or her know that your mare should foal soon. Once your mare's stall is clean and well bedded, hook up your foaling cam and watch for the next stage.

Stage I: Labor.

What you'll see: As your mare begins to go into labor, she'll appear restless—pacing in her stall, eating, and tossing bits of hay. She might paw the bedding and switch her tail. She might also get up and down, and urinate frequently. This stage usually lasts one to four hours.

What's happening: Your mare's cervix is *dilating* (opening) and she's experiencing contractions. The foal is starting to move, but the mare's water hasn't yet broken.

Foal position: The foal should now be aligned, with his spine close to the mare's spine. His front legs should be pointed toward the mare's hind end with his head resting on his knees, ready for delivery.

What to do: Get ready! Foaling is imminent.

Stage II: Water breaking and delivery.

What you'll see: Your mare's "water" will break—making a loud rushing sound. The amount of water in the *chorioallantoic sac* (the fluid-filled sac that surrounded the foal during gestation) far surpasses the amount of liquid she'd discharge while urinating. The liquid will look like urine, but will have a mild, non-offensive odor and will be tinted tan. Your mare may lie down, stand up, or keep moving as delivery progresses.

Next you'll see the amnionic sac appear outside your mare's vulva. Inside the white, glistening membrane, you'll see the foal's front hooves, soles down. One foot will be slightly in front of the other. As the foal's knees emerge, you should also see his nose. Your mare might rest a bit once the foal's head is out.

Your mare should lie down and stay down for the rest of delivery. In a few minutes, she'll push out the foal's shoulders—the widest part. Your foal should be on the ground within thirty minutes after the mare's water breaks.

What's happening: Your mare's chorioallantoic sac breaks, releasing the fluid that once surrounded the foal. Once the water breaks, your mare continues contracting, moving the foal to the birth canal and out. The foal's front legs edge out first as your mare continues delivery.

Foal position: The foal is pushed out as your mare's uterus contracts and her cervix dilates. He'll move out with his chin resting on his knees. As your mare continues to push, the foal will stretch out, lengthening his body and gradually sliding out the mare's vulva. His back hooves will emerge last.

Common problems: If you see something that doesn't match the typical birth explained above, call your veterinarian. You can help out in some cases, but your vet should be notified. Here are some common birthing problems:

- Your mare's water may not break. Instead, she may "red bag"—that is, she'll attempt to deliver the placenta with the chorioallantoic sac intact, after it's separated prematurely from the uterus. If this occurs, the foal won't have oxygen during delivery.
- Your mare may not lie down. Instead, she'll deliver while standing, causing the foal to fall headfirst to the ground.

Lenita Brahim takes a stroll with her hours-old foal at Poetry In Motion Arabians, Fresno, California. (photo by Zita)

- The foal may not present two front legs. Instead, you may see one leg, two legs with the soles up, two legs with no nose, two legs with the head on the cannon bones instead of the knees, two back legs, etc. This is known as *dystocia*—difficult birth.

What to do: If your mare appears to be progressing well, you may not have to intervene. However, if you notice anything different from what's normal, be on guard, and act quickly.

Here are several actions you can safely take:

- Take note of your mare's location. If she's too close to a wall, get her up, and move her toward the middle of the stall. If she delivers too close to the wall, the baby might get trapped and suffocate.

    "One of my clients walked into the barn just as a first-time mare was delivering standing up," Dr. Immegart recalls. "The foal was already falling. He tried to catch it in his arms, but the foal was slippery. Still, he saved it from falling headfirst by breaking its fall."

- If you see anything red and velvety coming from your mare's vulva ("red bag"), cut the bag with scissors or a knife. Be careful not to cut the foal.

- If you see any abnormal presentation, walk your mare, and call your veterinarian. Walking your mare will help slow her contractions—saving you time until your vet arrives to manipulate the foal's position.

- Your foal may be "elbow hung" if his nose comes out on his legs, but is too far forward. His head will rest on his cannon bones instead of his knees. If this happens, gently pull the legs forward. His elbows were caught behind the pelvic rim.

- If the foal's feet are perfectly even, gently pull one slightly ahead. This will angle his shoulders to allow him to come out more quickly and easily.

- If your mare takes a long break from pushing after the foal's head is out, break the sac so that the foal can breathe. If she doesn't start active labor again within ten to fifteen minutes, apply *gentle* traction to the foal's legs. "This isn't time for two guys and a tractor," Dr. Immegart warns. "One person with a tiny bit of pressure will stimulate her to start again. Gently wrap your hands around the foal's legs and slide your hands toward you in an outward and downward direction."

  What not to do: Don't try to change your foal's position without a veterinarian present unless you see your foal's front legs with hooves down and a nose. *Don't pull if you don't see a head.* "Your veterinarian will guide the fetus back in and turn it," Dr. Immegart says. "Anything but two feet with soles down and a head on knees is abnormal; call the vet."

- Don't pull on the foal's legs with the intent of pulling him out. You may rip your mare's cervix and cause internal damage if she hasn't dilated enough.

ABOUT THE PLACENTA

Save and examine your mare's placenta after foaling. You'll want to make sure the placenta is complete—thereby reducing the chance that your mare may founder or get an infection.

The placenta is made up of two membranes—the *amnion* (an opaque membrane that surrounds the foal in utero) and the *chorioallantois* (a membrane that joins the placenta to the uterus). Your veterinarian will examine the placenta to make sure it's free from tears and will also analyze its color.

If your mare was sick, or if your foal was sick or stillborn, save the placenta and any fetal remains for a laboratory test. Pack the placenta on ice, and ship it to your state's veterinary college or a well-known lab for testing. The placenta can provide valuable details to help you know what went wrong and what may need to be changed in the future.

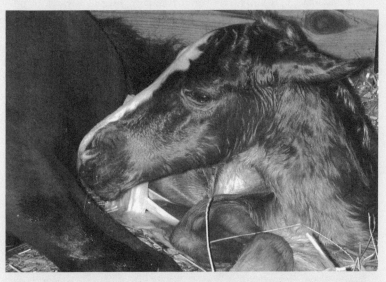

A newborn Rocky Mountain Horse foal takes his first breaths at Cedar Grove Farm, Peacham, Vermont. (photo by Mike Hartong)

Stage III: Delivering the placenta.

What you'll see: After the foal is out, your mare will most likely rest. She might even rest while the foal's back legs are still in the birth canal. In a few minutes, she'll stand and the umbilical cord will break. The foal may bleed a bit from his umbilical cord.

Your mare will begin to lick the foal to dry him. At the same time, the foal will attempt to stand. He'll fall down several times before standing on wobbly legs. As he stands, he'll look for his mother's teats and begin to nurse. Soon after eating, he'll pass *meconium* (the first excrement).

Your mare may begin to deliver the placenta. She might look uncomfortable and somewhat colicky after birth and before placenta delivery. She might kick at her belly and look at her barrel. However, unlike colic, she'll want to eat. Within three hours, the placenta should be pushed out.

What's happening: As mare and foal begin to move, the umbilical cord stretches and tears. "It's nature's way of making sure it doesn't bleed too much," Dr. Immegart says. "The vessels recoil and contract so that too much blood doesn't come through."

At Cedar Grove Farm, a prescription for health: fresh air, sunshine, and green grass. (photo by Mike Hartong)

As the foal gains strength and stands, he'll start to suckle. This stimulates the mare to begin contractions to expel the placenta. The mare begins contractions again, which cause abdominal discomfort. She soon delivers the placenta, thereby expelling all materials from the pregnancy.

The foal will produce his first fecal material. The material is made up of all the material that passed through his system in utero.

COMMON PROBLEMS

Retained placenta.

Pulling on the placenta to get it out in a hurry can cause major problems. Retained placentas occur when part of the placenta remains in the uterus. The placenta is made up of tiny membranes, which tear easily. Pulling causes tears and can lead to uterine infections, and even laminitis and founder.

Uterine prolapse.

In rare cases, your mare may experience *uterine prolapse* (part of the uterus gets pulled into itself). If your mare prolapses, she'll have colic symptoms. She'll also have poor gum color. This can be a side effect of giving too much oxytocin. Pulling on the placenta can also cause the uterus to prolapse. Call your veterinarian if your mare doesn't want to eat after delivering.

Passing meconium.

Many foals have trouble passing meconium on their own. They might strain or raise their tails without result.

What to do:

- Allow your mare and foal time to rest after birth.
- Administer an enema to your foal if he has trouble passing meconium. Take a 60cc catheter-tip syringe and fill it with warm, soapy water. The solution will be milder than an over-the-counter enema. However, you may also use the store-bought variety. Lift your foal's tail and gently administer two syringes full—120cc. Be gentle, and never apply pressure. (For details, see chapter 13.) If the fecal material doesn't appear, call your veterinarian.

- Administer oxytocin if your mare has a history of laminitis, or if the placenta hasn't delivered within three hours.
- On the advice of your veterinarian, administer Banamine (a common nonsteroidal anti-inflammatory medication) if your mare looks uncomfortable after birth and before she delivers the placenta.
- In any case, call your veterinarian, and announce your foal's birth. He or she might want to check your foal for *immunoglobulin* (antibodies produced by white blood cells during an immune response) that should've been passed to him through the mare's colostrum.

"I don't need to see the foal the moment it hits the ground, but I do need to see it that day—even if everything went okay," Dr. Immegart says. "I want to make sure there was adequate colostrum. I do a simple blood test for immunity. If there's some reason to believe the foal didn't get his immunity, I can give the foal what he needs with plasma. You're making sure that the foal is protected against infectious diseases when you check immunity soon after birth."

What not to do:

- Don't rush in to "cut the cord" as soon as the foal is on the ground. The umbilical cord should break by itself. You only need to act if the foal is bleeding excessively.
- Never force an enema.
- Never pull on the placenta.

Sweet dreams: El Miladi Zareena at El Miladi Arabian Stud, Carrizozo, New Mexico.
(photo by Richard T. Bryant)

CHAPTER THIRTEEN

YOUR FOAL'S FIRST TWENTY-FOUR HOURS

Peaceful contentment: La Kelila and Lasalle Jullyen V at Varian Arabians.
(photo by Zita)

191

'MILK ANYONE?'

A couple of years ago, a beautiful, young mare we own had her first foal, a fine-looking colt. We were delighted. But soon, our emotions were tempered, because although he nursed normally, she wasn't producing enough milk to sustain him.

Fortunately, we work with a woman who provides nurse mares just for situations like this. However, when we caught up with her on her cell phone, she was on the road several states distant, with a broken-down truck. She promised us a nurse mare, but cautioned it might be two days before she could deliver one. Meanwhile, we had to decide how to feed young Imperial Kagaan.

Sometimes, one can coax a newborn foal to drink milk from a bucket. While they'll take a bottle more readily, there's the chance that the foal might aspirate the liquid into his lungs. This can lead to a mechanical pneumonia, which can become a more serious bacterial pneumonia.

Rather than that, we decided to find a willing veteran mare that had just foaled and see whether she'd mind an extra mouth to feed. We waited until our target mare's own offspring was napping, and brought in little Kagaan. She welcomed him readily! He had a long drink, and we thought it was very cute that the mare nickered softly after him when we took him away.

Kagaan had to nurse every hour around the clock, so eventually we had four mares nursing him along. Every mare we asked sweetly welcomed him—not one pinned her ears. After a while, we didn't even bother to hold the mare. Once in a while, the mare's own offspring would awake, and both foals would nurse at the same time.

It was three days before the nurse mare arrived, but Kagaan didn't miss a meal. In fact, he adapted with ease. He'd merrily trot behind us down the barn aisles and, without hesitation, would follow us into a stall for his supper. Today, he's one of the most sociable, well-adjusted youngsters we have, and one day will be a handsome replacement for his sire.

We'll always treasure memories of Kagaan's unique start in life, courtesy of four generous surrogate mothers. We probably should've hung a sign around his neck: "Got Milk?"

—Beverly Sziraky, manager, Imperial Egyptian Stud, Parkton, Maryland

Congratulations! Your long-anticipated, carefully planned foal has arrived on the planet. The birth was uncomplicated, and both mare and foal are resting comfortably. Now what? The next twenty-four hours couldn't be more important. In most instances, nature presides, and horses are better without our interference. However, if anything adverse should happen, it's critical that you spot it early, and act or call your veterinarian pronto. Both mare and foal have been through a stressful, demanding experience, and if things go wrong, the situation can deteriorate quickly.

To help guide us through the foal's vital first twenty-four hours, we went to Dave Sauter, DVM. Dr. Sauter completed a veterinary internship at the noted Rood & Riddle Equine Hospital in Lexington, Kentucky, before settling at Kulshan Veterinary Hospital in Lyndon, Washington.

"After the mare's prolonged pregnancy, when nothing happens quickly, the delivery and the time immediately afterward are a complete contrast—filled with dramatic events that progress rapidly," Dr. Sauter says. "Within a brief span of time, the foal goes from complete dependency on the placenta and womb, to running and jumping on its four legs! It's amazing to witness. Your attentiveness during this critical period will help ensure a positive outcome for both your mare and foal."

Read on, as Dr. Sauter explains the usual sequence of events, and when and how to intervene; common problems and how to address them; and what to expect at your foal's first physical exam.

After a Routine Delivery

"First, it's imperative that the foaling and post-foaling environment is a quiet, familiar haven for your mare," Dr. Sauter says. "I once had clients whose maiden mare delivered uneventfully. However, they immediately called neighbors to join them, turned on lots of lights to film the newborn, and excitedly started to celebrate. To the mare, which was experiencing the unsettling stress and pain of birth, these were strange people, voices, lights, and smells. She was frightened! She completely rejected her foal. In fact, she tried to kill the creature that she thought caused all the tumult—her foal."

So, maintain a quiet, safe environment as you attend the birth of your foal and witness the sweet tableau that follows, Dr. Sauter says, and be "like a tiny, silent mouse in the corner, watching events unfold." Save the celebratory song and dance for later.

"Remember the 'One-two-three Rule,' " Dr. Sauter says. "Note the time of birth. Usually, within one hour, the foal is up; in two hours, he'll be nursing; and in three hours, the placenta will be expelled from the mare. Since this is an average, if things take forty-five to sixty minutes longer, that's okay. However, beyond that, you should call your veterinarian."

In chronological order, here's what to expect, and what Dr. Sauter suggests you do:

- You may observe that after your mare has the final contraction and pushes out the foal's hips, she'll rest even though the newborn's hind legs are still in the birth canal. Don't disrupt the mare and foal at this time, because blood is still flowing from the placenta through the umbilical cord and into the foal. If you make a lot of commotion, she might stand too soon, breaking the cord before the blood has finished pumping.

BABY'S VITAL STATISTICS—THE FIRST FORTY-EIGHT HOURS OF LIFE

Respiratory rate: 60–80 breaths per minute the first two hours, stabilizing to 20–40 breaths per minute.
Heart rate: As high as 140 beats per minute the first two hours, stabilizing to 80–120 beats per minute by twelve hours.
Rectal temperature: As low as 98.6 degrees Fahrenheit at birth, warming to 100.4 by the end of the first hour. Normal range: 99–101 degrees Fahrenheit.
Time to standing: Average, one hour, but may be 60–180 minutes.
Time to sucking reflex: Average, 20 minutes, after foaling.
Nursing: First suckle by Hour 3, then every 15–30 minutes afterward.
Urination: First urination between Hours 4–8.
Bowel movements: After meconium passage, 8–10 times per day.

(It's a good idea to keep this posted near the foaling stall.)

- If you note, however, that the placenta is covering the foal's face and nostrils, then take action. As quietly as possible, enter the stall, and remove the placenta from the foal's nostrils, so he can breathe.

- Usually, the foal will sit upright on his sternum, and lift his head. Don't try to pull the foal's feet from the mare; normally, his movement within the first half-hour will do that naturally.

- Either the foal's movement or the mare's effort to stand will break the umbilical cord. This is the time to dip it in *dilute chlorhexidene.* Place the solution in a small paper cup, and hold it to the foal's

Here he comes! Imperial Kagaan, bred by Imperial Egyptian Stud, Parkton, Maryland. (photo by Cappy Jackson)

abdomen for five seconds. (Avoid other disinfectants; even "tamed" iodine can be too harsh and create problems.) Continue to do this twice a day for three days.

- On rare occasions, the umbilical cord will bleed inordinately. If it does, tie it off with clean fishing line or umbilical tape, or clamp it with a sterile *hemostat* (locking clamp). Call your veterinarian, so he or she can attend to the cord to prevent infection.

- Expect your foal to shiver even if it's warm outside. It's a natural reflex. However, if it's colder than 40 degrees, it's good to towel off the newborn. If your mare is very protective, you may need someone to gently hold her head while you dry the foal with a clean, fluffy towel.

- Many foals will display the sucking reflex within minutes of birth, and some precocious little guys will be up and nursing within thirty minutes. Generally, if they haven't latched onto mom within two hours, they need assistance. While one attendant holds the mare, you can try to gently ease the foal to the nipple. I've gone to the opposite side of the mare, and squirted some milk in his face. It works! If, however, this seems to confuse the foal, don't force it. If he isn't nursing by three hours, call your veterinarian. The foal needs the mare's vital *colostrum* (first milk), not just for energy, but for its vital antibodies that help protect against infection. If the foal is unable to accomplish a basic task like nursing, something may be seriously amiss.

- After your foal has had several good meals, he should have the strength to pass *meconium,* the first stool passed. The meconium isn't true feces, but a combination of cellular debris and firm mucus. Usually, it takes six or more bowel movements to pass the meconium. Because meconium impaction is a leading cause of colic in the foal, enemas are frequently prescribed. Discuss this in advance with your veterinarian, and see "How to Give an Enema."

- For the first few hours, your foal will do little else but nurse, sleep, and pass meconium. Sometimes, owners use imprinting techniques during this time. (See chapter 14.) However, it's vital not to interfere with the bonding between mare and foal. Barring emergency, the post-delivery veterinarian examination is best accomplished when the foal is twelve to eighteen hours old. (See "The First Veterinary Exam.")

HOW TO GIVE AN ENEMA

Now, Dr. Sauter answers commonly asked questions regarding the meconium and the administration of the enema, if recommended by your veterinarian.

What is meconium?

Meconium consists of glandular secretions, swallowed amniotic fluid, and other cellular debris. Before birth, it's stored in the colon and rectum. Meco-

Closely supervised by mom, this young Quarter Horse filly explores her new universe.
(photos by Heidi Nyland)

THE FIRST VETERINARY EXAM

After an uncomplicated birth, the mare and foal should be examined by your veterinarian within twelve to eighteen hours. Here's what he or she will look for:

- A complete placenta, with no sign of disease.
- Healthy heart, lungs, eyes.
- Pink gums, with capillary refill within one second.
- No hernias.
- Sound limbs.
- Passed meconium.
- Adequate colostrum absorption.

Expect both to have very good appetites. The foal will gain two to three pounds per day, all from his mother. Provide your mare high-quality hay, but no more grain than she's accustomed to eating. This isn't the time to introduce a new diet. After this wellness exam, Dr. Sauter offers his favorite prescription for the mare and foal, "Plenty of fresh air, green grass, and sunshine."

---

nium is usually dark brown to black, and may be found in hard pellets or may be in a more pastelike mass. One indication that all the meconium has passed is a change to light brown to yellowish color, and a change in consistency to more mucouslike.

How long does it take to pass the meconium?

Most foals start passing the meconium within a couple of hours of birth. Most foals start after they've nursed well for the first time. It seems the colostrum stimulates them to try to defecate. Occasionally, the urge to defecate interferes with their ability to nurse. Generally, all the meconium is passed within half a day.

Why is passage of meconium so important?

Meconium impaction is the most common cause of colic in the newborn foal. Meconium impaction generally responds to medical treatment, but sometimes, surgery is the only way to clear the impaction. Meconium impaction is

extremely stressful on the newborn, and is a major setback during a very critical and vulnerable
stage of life.

Should I give my foal an enema?

Medical opinions on the routine
use of enemas in newborn foals
vary. The intent is to *prevent*
meconium impaction and to *reduce* the straining and discomfort
associated with meconium passage. As with any type of procedure, there are risks involved. The
lining of the rectum in the foal is
thin, and can be bruised or even
torn by awkward, careless, or in-
appropriate administration. The
most important step is to properly

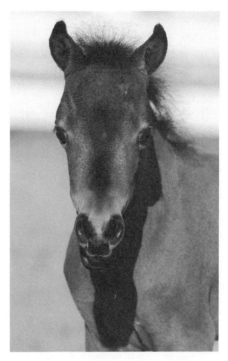

A sensational Miniature Horse colt.
(photo by Jay Goss)

restrain the foal. Administering an enema to a newborn isn't safe without restraint. (See below.)

How do I prepare an enema?

Prepare the enema ahead of time. At our veterinary hospital, we recommend
the Gentle-Tip Phosphate Enema. Warm the solution to about body temperature, much like warming a baby's bottle. (Tip: Test the solution on your
wrist to make sure it's not too hot.) Apply extra lubricant to the tip; K-Y Jelly
or a similar gynecological lubricant works well.

How do I restrain the newborn foal?

First, get a helper—this is definitely a two-person job. (In fact, it's helpful to
have a third person to keep your mare from interfering and calm her—some
mares will get upset when their foals are restrained.) One person should cradle

the foal's neck and gently force the foal against a wall with his or her body. The other person should stand on the same side of the foal, just in front of the foal's rear leg, facing the foal's hind end. This person should also gently force the foal toward the wall. This will limit the foal's avenues of escape.

What evasive tactics might the foal try?

There are three common foal evasive tactics you might encounter. First, he might suddenly—and repeatedly—*jerk his head* straight up. Make sure your (or your helper's) nose isn't in the way. Second, the foal might take a *sudden leap* forward. If you (or your helper) don't have a firm hold on the foal, he might jump out of your arms. Third, the foal might *collapse,* as though unconscious. This is often followed by a sudden leap, especially if you allow him to fall down to the ground. Be prepared for these behaviors. Support the foal with firm restraint, and quickly but safely administer the enema.

How do I give the foal an enema?

Assuming you're the person at the foal's hind end, carefully grab the foal's tail, and elevate it *straight up* and forward, toward his head. It's important to lift the tail straight up and forward—don't move it to the side. With your other hand, *gently* insert the enema into the rectum, and squeeze out the entire contents. *Never* force the enema into the rectum—it should slide without any obstruction, almost effortlessly. Note that some liquid might spray out as you get to the end. Using *kind* but *firm* restraint will minimize the struggling, and make the procedure *faster* and *safer* for everyone.

Should I give a second enema?

Always consult your veterinarian before administering a second enema. One enema is preventive and helpful. A second enema can be very irritating.

POST-FOALING PROBLEMS

"The following are problems I encounter most frequently," Dr. Sauter says. "But there are a wide variety of difficulties, some extremely serious, some not. One of the best things an owner can do is use common sense: If something doesn't seem quite right, call your veterinarian immediately."

Here's a rundown of common post-foaling problems provided by Dr. Sauter.

Retained placenta.

As I mentioned earlier, the placenta should be expelled from the mare completely within three hours. If this doesn't happen, veterinary intervention is necessary. *Always* collect the placenta, and put it in a bucket of cold water for your veterinarian to examine when he or she arrives for the post-delivery examination. *Never* attempt to remove the placenta

A captivating filly bred by Dr. Robert Freele, Houston, Texas. (photo by Randi Clark)

from your mare by pulling it out! It's attached to the uterus, and pulling can cause dangerous hemorrhage. Don't tear portions still on the foal from what's still inside the mare—this is counterproductive, because the weight helps cause the placenta to be expelled.

A night attendant at a foaling center taught me an old trick: When a large portion of the placenta had been torn off in birth, he'd tie a small plastic bag filled with a quart of grain to the remaining placenta inside the mare. This simulated the weight lost when the placenta tore (and isn't excessive), and would help the mare expel it.

However, it's best to call your vet. In just six hours, retained placenta can cause a serious, potentially life-threatening infection, which will require antibiotics.

Postpartum pain.

Postpartum pain (pain that occurs after foaling) can be overwhelming for a mare, especially first-time mothers. Although it may seem like the severe

FOAL-REJECTION CURE?

Brenda and Stuart Schuettpelz own Tuscani Arabians in Niles, Michigan. Brenda, a third-generation horse breeder, observes every foaling from a foal cam, always ready to assist, but careful not to intrude. She's studied foal rejection, and has some interesting observations.

"I've interviewed breeders who've had problems with rejecter mares, especially their maiden mares," Schuettpelz says. "Many times, it turned out that the placenta was removed from the stall immediately. In some cases, the breeders had removed the placenta because the mare was trying to eat it. Later, with our encouragement, some of these breeders have bred these mares again, leaving the placenta in the stall for the second foaling. If the mare wanted to lick the placenta, the breeder let her have it. After the mare sniffed, licked, or bit the placenta, she turned around, and sniffed and licked the foal." This time the mare didn't reject her foal!

"While I don't think this is a cure-all for all rejecter mares," notes Brenda, "I believe a certain populous of rejecter mares are created by the early removal of the placenta or afterbirth from the mares' foaling area—often combined with pain-management issues.

"With some maiden mares on our farm, after the mare has had a good once-over with the placenta, we've put the placenta in a five-gallon pail of cold sterile water to preserve the placenta [for the vet to inspect]," Brenda continues. "Then we cut a patch of the placenta and put it in the middle of the foals' back, for the mares to lick and sniff. The mares' reactions have been a grunt, squeal, or low nicker, after they sniff what we call 'the patch.' But right afterward, they present themselves to the foals for nursing. This has helped us stimulate their nurturing instincts when we've had a foal that's slow to nurse. It's helped them bond. If the patch dries out, we have a fresh source of new patches in the bucket. One of our maiden mares took three days of patches to bond, but it was certainly preferable to rejection!"

Far fetched? Actually, Dave Sauter, DVM, says this technique is often used to introduce nurse mares to orphan or rejected foals. Additionally, Schuettpelz directs us to a February 2005 bulletin from the University at Buffalo (www.buffalo.edu/news/fast-execute.cgi/article-page.html?article=71210009), titled *Ingestion of Afterbirth Appears to Promote Maternal Behavior in Mammals*. Mark Kristal, PhD, a UB professor of psychology and director of the graduate program in behavior neuroscience, has received a grant from the National Science Foundation to test his premise. Developments in his fascinating research may well aid in the prevention of foal rejection.

abdominal pain of colic, postpartum pain originates from uterine contractions. I prescribe Banamine (a nonsteroidal anti-inflammatory medication) on a case-by-case basis. This severe pain may come on without warning. A mare will suddenly look extremely tight in the flanks and go down to roll. Once, I was dipping a foal's navel, when his dam literally dropped to the ground and rolled, her leg just missing hitting my head. You and your veterinarian should plan in advance how to handle the possibility of postpartum pain.

Foal rejection.

It's my experience that fear is a significant factor in a mare's rejection of her foal. Birth is a confusing, painful experience, and she can become fearful of something unfamiliar, such as the placenta, or even her foal. If your mare tries to injure the foal, remove him from danger immediately. Call your veterinarian, because you'll need to address both his immediate nutritional needs and longtime care.

There are steps you can take to prevent rejection, especially with the maiden mare. Make her foaling environment as safe and familiar as possible. If you're planning to have her foal at your veterinarian's facility or the stallion station, get her settled in at least a month prior to her foaling date. Long before the birth, we have attendants enter the mare's stall two, then three times per night, so she's used to the company. And we try to desensitize her to being touched and handled, so our veterinary prodding won't offend her.

Insufficient quantity or quality of colostrum.

As mentioned earlier, the colostrum contains vital antibodies that safeguard the foal from infection. A newborn has no protection, but during the first twelve hours of life, he can absorb these antibodies directly through his gastrointestinal tract into his bloodstream. That ability begins to decline after twelve hours, and is gone by twenty-four hours. If a mare has been dripping milk for days before the birth, she might not have quality colostrum. Or, if the foal doesn't nurse adequately, he may not get the quantity he needs. With poor-quality colostrum, if there's just not enough, *failure of passive transfer* (FTP) occurs and the foal is vulnerable to disease and infection. When your veterinarian examines the foal at twelve to eighteen hours, he or she will test

Expressive and engaged with life: Varian Arabians' Sweet Siesta V with her daughter. (photo by Zita)

RAISING AN ORPHAN

Ann Myers of Myers Horse Farms, Ashland, Ohio, has bred champion Quarter Horses for nearly twenty-five years. Twice, she's raised orphan foals whose mothers died shortly after their birth. Both times, the foals received colostrum from their dams, augmented from an emergency supply Myers keeps in the barn freezer.

With no nurse mare available, Myers then easily taught the orphan foals to drink high-quality replacement milk from a bucket; such milk is readily available at the local feed store. "Milk replacement is usually formulated to feed cool and slightly bitter," Myers says. "If you feed the milk too warm and sweet, foals gulp it down—too much all at once—and they'll get diarrhea. It's far better for them to drink little bits, but often."

Myers owns an "itty bitty" pony that helped socialize the orphans and kept them company in their stalls. "We had to be careful that the little gelding didn't scarf up the foals' milk and feed, because he'd gladly do that, too. But he's a wonderful babysitter, who absolutely loves to play with the babies."

During the day, as Myers worked in the barn, she often opened the orphans' stall doors, so they could roam the aisles, and peek into other stalls to see the other horses.

"It was really cute," Myers says. "They were a little like puppy dogs, and to see the look of surprise on their faces when they saw full-sized horses, I sometimes wondered if they knew they *were* horses! As you can imagine, they both grew up very attached to humans. They loved to see us coming, were very responsive, and loved all the attention they got."

As they matured, were the orphans different than other foals? "Because they were very socialized to us, initially when they were turned out with their own species, they acted like, 'Yikes! This must be a mistake!' But of course they adapted. Later, both relaxed and adjusted to training easily. They were both very willing partners, with particularly happy dispositions."

An epilogue: One orphan grew up to become a hunt seat futurity champion at the All American Quarter Horse Congress; the other, a reserve American Quarter Horse Association world champion junior Western pleasure horse.

the foal's antibody level in the blood. If necessary, your vet will provide supplemental colostrum.

Retained meconium.

As mentioned earlier, after nursing a few times, the foal will pass meconium. Because foals have very narrow pelvises, the hard, compacted balls of meconium can get jammed there. While we routinely prescribe enemas, giving an enema to a delicate foal is a two-person procedure. (For details, see "How to Give an Enema.") Don't delay, because after six to twelve hours, retained meconium is more complicated, and can be life-threatening. By then, stomach tubes and intravenous fluids are required.

Impaction in the mare.

We also like to see the mare pass a stool within twelve hours of birth. Sometimes, the delivery and pelvic bruising will cause problems. Your veterinarian can help by administering mineral oil by *nasal-gastric tube* (one that runs through the nasal passages and into the stomach).

Septicemia.

This is a bacterial infection of the bloodstream, acquired either before or immediately after birth. The foal may be infected through the umbilical cord, or the gastrointestinal or respiratory tracts. Some signs include elevated heart rate, elevated respiration, bloodshot eyes, lethargy, colic, and diarrhea. If you even suspect septicemia, call your veterinarian immediately. Your foal needs emergency care.

Asphyxia.

This is due to a decrease in the foal's supply of oxygen, usually related to his birth. While foals may be stillborn or struggling at birth, ones that appear normal may still develop problems as long as twenty-four hours after birth. Some causes are delay in delivery, congenital abnormalities, and illness in the mare. Signs may include spasms, jerky movements, seizures, wandering, even coma. Sometimes, these foals may be nursed back to health.

I'll never forget the Thoroughbred colt, whose maiden mother had a very difficult foaling experience. The colt suffered oxygen debt and was in a coma. It was February, and quite cold, so we put him in the corner of the stall with heat lamps above and an electric blanket over him. We gave him intravenous fluids, and fed him through a gastric tube. And we rotated his body so he didn't get "bed sores." Four days after his birth, he came out of his coma.

Unfortunately, by the time the foal came out of his coma, his dam—who had significant health challenges, too—lost interest, because the foal had never nursed. But we put him on a wonderful nurse mare, and the colt made a complete recovery. Not every case of asphyxia has a happy ending, but this one absolutely did.

Limb abnormalities.

Call your veterinarian immediately if the foal has visible abnormalities of the legs, such as crooked legs, contracted tendons, or overly lax tendons. Many of these problems can be corrected with prompt veterinary attention.

There are lessons to be learned, and often mother knows best! (photo by Zita)

YOUR FOALING KIT

About a month before your mare's due date, collect the items you'll need to have on hand when she delivers. You, an experienced foaling attendant, or your veterinarian will find these items helpful both for normal deliveries and to help address foaling problems.

Collect the following in a clean box:

Sterile sleeves (disposable)
Surgical gloves
KY Jelly
Surgical scissors
Stethoscope
Specimen cups
Fleet enema
Thermometer

Also have on hand:

Clean towels
Distilled water
Nolvasan solution or iodine
Alcohol
Syringes and needles
Normal saline (at least four quarts)
Rolled cotton
Hot/cold water supply
Stainless steel bucket and bucket liners (small trash bags)
Ivory soap
Lubiseptic (antibacterial cleansing solution)
Foal blanket
Heat lamps, radiant heaters, or other safe means of raising the
    temperature of the foaling area
Foal Resuscitator
Foaling Predictor Kit
Colostrometer (determines the specific gravity of colostrum
    obtained immediately post-partum)

—Courtesy of Imperial Egyptian Arabians, Parkton, Maryland

CHAPTER FOURTEEN

BONDING WITH BABY

A comely youngster at Varian Arabians. (photo by Zita)

COLD PIZZA, ANYONE?

It was a beautiful, late July afternoon, and our foaling barn, with its portico with a table and chairs, was the perfect place to enjoy a light supper while waiting for my favorite broodmare to foal. My husband, Vaughn, had just left to deliver some shipped semen to the airport, so I phoned in an order to the local pizza delivery, and relaxed to watch a fiery-colored sunset.

Our mare, Daheda, was in the barn's front stall, so close I could hear her walking around on the straw. No sooner had I sat down than I heard her water break. Immediately, I went inside, and found her lying down. A tiny little nose and one foot were starting to emerge. But no other foot! It was bent back at the knee.

Quickly, I ran to our laboratory next door, called our veterinarian, and told him the presentation wasn't right. He replied that he was on his way.

I went back to Daheda, and got her up onto her feet. With that, the foal slipped back inside the birth canal. My heart was pounding, and the adrenaline flowing. I put my arm inside her, and slowly, gently, brought the folded leg around and forward. Experience told me that the leg was now presented correctly.

A veteran mother, Daheda laid back down, and this time, the little muzzle and two tiny feet came out. Within minutes, the entire foal was out, the sac was off, and before me was a perfect, chestnut colt. Both he and his mother were just fine. I admit to shedding a few tears as I kissed his precious little nose!

Right about then, the vet's van screeched to a stop outside the barn, followed in rapid succession by my husband and the pizza delivery man. As each arrived at the stall, I looked around to see varying looks of joy and surprise on their faces. As you might've guessed, our pizza was cold by the time we got around to it, but it still tasted great.

Over the years, that colt, True Colours, has gone on to collect show championships in the United States and Europe, and now is siring another generation of champions. We share a special bond—and he still loves to have his nose kissed.

—Victoria Snelgrove, Source Arabians International, Ontario, Canada

WHEN YOUR LONG-AWAITED FOAL FINALLY ARRIVES ON THE planet, you likely can hardly wait to establish a relationship with him. During the previous eleven months, you might've daydreamed about riding the perfect reining pattern, sailing over jumps of enormous height and breadth, or heading down meandering trails through spectacular settings—all this, of course, on the horse of your dreams. But now that your fantasy foal is a living, breathing creature before you, where to begin? How to bond with baby?

We are not the first to seek a bond with our horses, Cynthia Culbertson of El Miladi Arabian Stud reminds us. "The Native Americans would softly speak to the belly of their mare before she foaled, so the newborn would know the sound of their voice. And it is said that the Bedouins of Arabia would receive the newborn foal in their arms, and caress them all over. Then, they would carry the foal around their camp, to accustom them to the sounds and smells. Afterward, the foal was considered a part of the tribe."

In previous chapters, we've noted what you should do to ensure the health and well-being of the newborn foal. But in this age of increased awareness of the partnership between horse and human, and the benefits of that bond, we find ourselves seeking ways to lay the foundation for the partnership at the very beginning of our horses' lives.

More than twenty years ago, Robert M. Miller, DVM, created a stir with the publication of his book, *Imprint Training of the Newborn Foal.* (For a complete listing of Dr. Miller's books and videos, visit www.robertMmiller .com.) The day-to-day experiences of his practice prompted him to consider the long-term impact and potential benefits of immediate human contact with the newborn. He first imprinted a foal forty-five years ago. Today, he explains:

"Nearly a half-century ago, as a young veterinarian just starting to practice, the births that took place in the earliest morning hours gave me invaluable opportunity for observation. Usually after a birth, and with the clock nearing four, there was neither reason nor time to go home and back to bed. So I'd just hang around with the new mother and foal, massaging the foal all over its body, and giving it a thorough physical, an enema, and the usual injections.

"Eventually, I'd leave for my office. But when I returned a day or even a week later for their follow-up examination, I'd notice that the foals I'd handled at birth seemed friendlier, and more docile and unafraid of human contact than the youngsters that weren't touched and stroked by humans immediately after birth. Some even seemed to recognize me. I started to wonder, just how important was all of this early handling?"

Dr. Miller's imprinting techniques are concentrated on the first hour of the foal's life, when the foal has a remarkable ability to learn. He also advocates additional sessions during the days following the birth to reinforce the imprinting lessons and add new experiences.

In imprinting, Dr. Miller believes that repeated rubbing of the body, face, ears, feet, legs, etc., desensitizes the foal, and allows the foal to easily accept and submit to a variety of situations throughout the rest of his life, from farrier trims to veterinary calls. This gentles the foal and lays the foundation for his partnership with humans.

A bright-eyed Morgan youngster at Fire Run Farm. (photo by Jay Goss)

For some horse breeders, Dr. Miller's book articulated what they already knew, perhaps even practiced in varying degrees. (See "In Touch with Horses.") For others, however, his techniques took early assistance and caress into the realm of interference between mother and newborn, and in inexperienced hands, potentially dangerous practices.

There *is* common ground, however, shared by both sides. Most agree that some early handling of the foal helps lay a foundation for the partnership between horse and human to follow. It can make everyday activities easier to accomplish without resistance, from cleaning horses' hooves and shoeing, to veterinary examinations and schooling lessons.

To learn more, we asked some veteran horsemen how they handle their newborn foals. What routine works for them? Where do they draw the line between assistance and interference? And what benefits do they reap from early efforts to bond with their baby?

MAMA KNOWS BEST

Vaughn and Victoria Snelgrove, the hands-on owners of Source Arabians International in Ontario, Canada, stand several stallions, and each year welcome numerous foals into the world. Victoria, who assists with both their mares and their clients' mares foaling, doesn't imprint, per se. During normal deliveries and afterward, she takes her cues from the mares, proceeds cautiously, and dispenses lots of loving care.

Snelgrove approaches each foaling situation individually, above all with respect for the most important bond—the bond between the mare and her foal. She divides the mares into two groups: maiden (first-time mothers) and veteran mares.

"For the maiden mare, this new experience is particularly stressful, not to mention painful," she says. "I've discovered that for them, less is best. I make sure everything proceeds as it should, and do the essentials (see chapter 13), but for the most part, I don't make my presence felt.

"New mothers might just decide, 'Okay, you love that pesky little thing so much, it's yours.' And we don't want that!" With maiden mares, Snelgrove handles their youngsters lovingly but minimally for the first two to three days. Then, with the mare and foal deeply bonded, she becomes more hands-on.

She finds veteran mares much more calm and complacent. "They usually welcome our presence, and once a foal is up and nursing, I go in to handle him, and give him some love." Years ago, Snelgrove says, one veteran mare taught her some essentials about bonding with baby, which she faithfully incorporates into her routine today:

1. Never box a foal into a corner, and always allow him access to his dam. That will keep both mare and foal confident and calm.

2. Don't rush, push, chase, or force yourself upon the foal—that stimulates the fright/flight response. Instead, try to wait until he looks to you, then get close to him. Make your actions slow and deliberate.

3. A mare will nibble on her foal's butt and tickle the top of his croup, which triggers the sucking and seeking response. Tickle your foal, too; he'll love it.

4. Gently rub and caress your foal as much as possible. Babies' bodies are sensitive, and they enjoy it. Pick up your foal's tiny feet, and lightly tap on his hooves; this will help prepare him for your farrier.

5. Be careful of your foal's neck. While I might slip a halter on and off, I don't attempt to lead with a halter during the first week. A foal's neck is fragile, and if he resists, you might have an accident on your hands.

6. Instead, "cradle" the foal to guide him: Stand on his left side, circle your right arm around his rump, and hug his chest with your left arm. Practice this technique in the stall first, before using it outside in the barn aisle or paddock. Once your foal learns this technique, you'll find it has many applications. I've used cradling months later, when I'm weaning foals. If they're upset about leaving their dams, cradling helps relax and comfort them. I've also used it to help calm yearlings while their feet are being trimmed.

7. After you've introduced a halter, adding a rump rope is usually no problem, because it's similar to cradling.

DREAM PARTNERSHIP

Horsewoman Jeanette Sandwald of Sequim, Washington, is a hearty advocate of Dr. Miller's techniques. She believes that her pinto Tennessee Walking

Life is full of new friends, new adventures. (photos by Zita)

In Touch with Horses

Day 1: Robert M. Miller, DVM, performs a birth imprinting session, teaching the foal to flex laterally, while the mare bonds with her newborn.
(All sidebar photos by Mrs. Robert Miller)

When Robert M. Miller, DVM, was still in veterinary school, he spent summers working as a wrangler on ranches in the West, in wild mustang country. He still remembers what happened when, nearing the end of a long day in the saddle, he spotted a mustang mare in the distance. She was on the ground after delivering a foal. He suspected the birth had been within the past hour. He could see the placenta still hanging out of the mare, and the foal attempting to stand. Wobbling, the foal dropped back to the ground, but with the next attempt, he found his feet.

Dr. Miller was downwind from the scenario, so he watched, undetected, while the sun dropped low in the sky. Eventually, the mare stood, and the foal sought his first meal. Finally, Dr. Miller knew he had to continue back to the barn. As he and his horse started off, the mare's head whipped around at the movement, and she caught her first glimpse of her observer.

"Immediately, she whirled and raced at speed to join her herd," Dr. Miller says. "The foal bounced behind her, looking like a 'daddy longlegs,' trying to keep up with his mother. He was just a couple of hours old—how could he respond so easily? It's one of the marvels of nature."

Dr. Miller tells us that the horse is a *precocial species*; that is, at birth, his senses are advanced, and he's neurologically mature. In the wild, this is imperative to his survival and helps explain why a foal, shortly after birth, is bonded to his dam and able to flee from danger at full speed with her.

He describes the two to three hours immediately following birth as the foal's "critical learning time," when information is absorbed readily and retained permanently. Those hours represent the window for imprint training; the next three days are best for reinforcing this information by repetition and adding details. Instead of thinking of humans as predators, the foal will think of you as his leader or the lead horse. Your bond with him and the attitudes he develops last for the rest of his life. Horses never forget anything.

Day 2: Reinforcing yesterday's lessons, the colt is indifferent to being "sacked out" with Dr. Miller's bandanna.

Dr. Miller also tells us that horses are the only domestic animal with flight as their first natural response to fear. His imprint handling is meant to desensitize the foal to frightening objects—such as plastic tarps, clippers, newspapers, and hair dryers—and reduce the flight response. Because of that, he says, many individuals involved in the racehorse industry protested that this technique would reduce their horses' capabilities.

"I think that with time and experience, they've come around," Dr. Miller says. "I've been to Thoroughbred farms that previously had rodeos when it was time to deworm their yearlings. They'd twitch the horses, and even then it was a battle. After imprinting— it was an entirely different story. It makes life just so much easier for trainers and veterinarians." And without negatively impacting the horses' running potential.

Dr. Miller says that four things happen when one imprints the foal:

- The foal bonds with the individual and even weeks later will recognize that person, and feel safe with them. There's a visual attachment.
- The foal will be desensitized to normally frightening stimuli, such as tarps, clippers, etc.
- The foal will be sensitized to human requests, such as flexion of the neck and legs, gentle tapping on hoof soles, etc.
- The foal will recognize the human as the dominant individual. Dr. Miller observes that mares push and touch their foals. This control of the youngsters' movement establishes the dominance hierarchy. Dr. Miller isn't aware of any other species that do so.

There are mistakes to be made, he cautions. Don't rush the initial session, he says, adding, "Don't stop if the foal offers resistance—you'll reward him and reinforce the flight response."

And after the first imprinting session, don't have a second session until the foal is more coordinated—perhaps as much as twenty-four hours later. Then limit subsequent sessions to a maximum of fifteen minutes. Physically, foals tire easily when they're standing. (As opposed to when they're lying down, when they don't fatigue and their attention span is limitless.)

Today, retired from his veterinary practice, Dr. Miller presents clinics on imprinting and natural horsemanship around the world, from Kenya to Japan, Poland to Patagonia. It was in Patagonia that he encountered his most skeptical audience of all: gauchos, with their long tradition of horsemanship—but, he reports, significant superstition and doubt.

"I gave a seminar there, on a large cattle station, with over two thousand horses," he says. "I set up my videos, but also insisted on using a live, five-hour-old foal with his dam. That Criole Horse was the fastest learner I've ever had! He only took about thirty minutes to relax and respond to imprinting. Then, the next day, we reassembled, and I demonstrated how gentle the foal was, and how he'd retained everything we'd taught him. They could hardly believe it.

"Later, their foreman came to me, and said, 'Thank you, I know you do this from the goodness of your heart. This completely changes our way of thinking.' And I told him, 'I didn't do this for you—I did it for your horses.'"

Day 5: Mr. Miller gently picks up the colt's hind leg with a loop of rope. There's no panic, just a quiet, relaxed response.

Horse gelding, Kelly, is a testament to the benefits of imprinting. When he was born eight years ago, she quickly developed a strong, trusting bond with the newborn that helped pull him through the challenging three weeks that followed.

Prior to the foaling date, Sandwald purchased Dr. Miller's video, *Imprint Training of the Newborn Foal,* and viewed it nearly half a dozen times. When her time came, Sandwald's mare, Cinnamon, foaled as so many mares do, in a brief period when her doting owner had taken a break. Sandwald returned to find the colt up and nursing. She retrieved the placenta and kept it for the veterinarian to examine. When the colt finished nursing, she doctored him. Then he lay down to rest, and she gently began the imprinting techniques, touching and rubbing the colt all over his body.

"Cinnamon had already bonded with him, and she readily accepted my presence," Sandwald says. "I was careful not to block her access to him, and she talked to him as I held him. He loved the handling and didn't offer any resistance. After the first time, I repeated the handling in sessions fifteen minutes in length, with at least four uninterrupted hours between sessions when he nursed and rested."

Sandwald called her veterinarian to have him come for the vital first examination. She'd also noticed with some dismay that her colt stood not on his front feet, but with his feet knuckled-over, standing on his fetlock joints. She speculates that the big-bodied colt had folded them over in the cramped space of the womb.

The condition, known as *contracted tendons,* has also been linked to a mineral imbalance in the dam and her diet. Treated early, youngsters usually fully recover. Sandwald's veterinarian constructed tiny braces and bandaged them to the colt's forelegs. The braces would help lengthen and straighten the contracted tendons.

But nothing seemed to dampen the little guy's spirits. He nursed heartily and slept deeply. Sandwald took several days off from work, and continued to handle her colt every four hours using Dr. Miller's techniques. He welcomed her and relaxed completely in her arms.

Sandwald also removed the braces twice a day, for eighteen days. With them off, she massaged the foal's legs. And, resting his hoof on her thigh, she gently pulled the leg straight, stretching the tendon. Before she replaced the braces with fresh bandages, she padded any areas of potential abrasion.

"The day I removed his braces for the last time, he took off running and prancing across the pasture, while I sat down and cried," she says. "Between imprinting and doctoring him, he and I developed a deep bond of trust that persists to this day. When we're on the trail and get into a tight situation, all I do is speak to him or touch his neck, and mentally he's right with me. He never panics. We have the kind of partnership I've always dreamed of having."

LESSONS OF A LIFETIME

Shawn Crews is general manager at Arabians Ltd., in Waco, Texas, where they've been breeding beautiful babies since 1977. Crews and foaling manager Patti Daniels attend the birth of nearly thirty foals each year.

"After the mare stands and the umbilical cord is broken, we medicate the cord, freshen the straw, and possibly towel the foal gently, but then we stand

UNDAUNTED SPIRIT

Years ago, my Arabian mare produced a charming filly. The mare was an exceptional athlete, and from her first steps, her daughter, Shakurah (which means "thankful" in Arabic), revealed an inclination to run and jump and prance. Unfortunately, when she was just two months old, she blithely ran into some very big trouble.

It had rained buckets that morning, but by afternoon, Shakurah joyously scampered around the pasture. After one "airs above the ground" maneuver, she touched down and cut directly into the path of her mother, who was running alongside her. In the slippery footing, the mare scrambled, but lost her balance—and despite her best efforts to avoid it, fell onto her daughter, breaking both of the filly's tiny hind legs.

At the time, it was my good fortune to live within driving distance of Auburn University. Shakurah went directly into surgery. On one leg, the talented veterinary surgeons pinned the head of the femur into the hip socket; on the other, they cast and taped together the hock.

The prognosis wasn't encouraging: The surgeons couldn't recall a case where a horse had survived two broken hind legs. They told me everything would depend on the little filly's attitude.

Shakurah woke in a stall with her mother, where both faced a three-month confinement. The mare easily could've been restless or bored and taken her frustration out on the filly. Instead, she never tired of showering love on her daughter. And Shakurah, despite everything, never lost her bright eyes.

Walking down the hospital aisles, I saw many young patients whose eyes were dulled by pain and circumstance. I vowed to put Shakurah out of her pain if the sparkle ever left her eyes—but it never did. When I peeked into her stall to say, "Good morning, baby girl," she'd always gleefully toss her head (about the only thing she could move), eyes flashing.

Shakurah survived the long confinement—and yet another when, as a yearling, the surgeons removed the pin from her femur. Twenty-one years later, she's still with me, and she still loves to trot and snort and buck.

Shakurah is a testament to the love of a mare for her foal, and the enormous courage and will to survive, even in one so small. And yes, her eyes still sparkle.

—*Cynthia Culbertson, El Miladi Arabian Stud, Carrizozo, New Mexico*

back and allow the new mother and her foal to bond. After the foal has nursed and obtained the important first milk, we'll caress his ears, legs, and feet, and talk to him. We don't poke our fingers into every orifice, however, I feel that's just too intrusive.

"I think it's critically important to continue your daily handling with at least fifteen to twenty minutes per day, for the next ten days. One of the worst things you can do is to handle them excessively the first day, then leave them alone. I've been with youngsters treated this way, and they're wild— like little jumping beans when it's time to wean them!"

Crews also mimics the horse's habit of scratching other horses at the withers—often seen in mutual grooming—to calm foals. She shares another technique that's handy to help relax apprehensive youngsters:

- While handling your foal and rubbing his body, place your finger at the corner of his mouth, and gently insert it. Massage his gums and tongue.
- When your foal makes chewing motions and relaxes, remove your finger. It won't take long.
- Continue to do this each bonding session. Remember to wait until he relaxes (sometimes foals will even take a deep breath) before you remove your finger.

"I've found this technique handy whenever a foal clenches his little jaws and seems uptight," Crews says. "It reassures and relaxes them. I've also used it later in their lives, when we're doing groundwork exercises and they get anxious for any reason. I'll put my finger in the corner of their mouth and massage the gums, and pretty soon, they're chewing and forgetting about anything scary. I also take that moment to think about how I'm presenting the lesson—perhaps I haven't been as clear as I could be. This technique is a wonderful aid throughout the horses' lives, whenever someone needs to deworm them or administer medication by mouth."

Common Sense—Makes Sense

The hours immediately following the birth offer us an extraordinary opportunity to bond with the baby. The examples of careful handling of the newborn that experienced horsemen have shared are all gentle in application, cautious in approach, and respectful of the all-important bond between mare and foal.

Just as prudent handling of the foal can lay the foundation for a partnership that lasts a lifetime, the overzealous or mismanaged handling of the newborn can also create problems with a challenging longevity. First-time horse breeders should remember:

- The mare's bond with her foal is paramount. To avoid possible foal rejection, don't push her away from her foal while you're handling him. Halter her, and have an assistant hold her nearby, where she can see what's going on. Usually, after the first one or two sessions, she'll accept your presence.
- Just as your handling will reinforce the positive, it can also strengthen a lasting negative impression. For example, when the foal is lying

Bonding with baby for a partnership that lasts a lifetime. (photo by Randi Clark)

down, and you flex its foreleg, don't release it if the youngster offers resistance. Gently and patiently continue to flex the leg until he relaxes and accepts. Otherwise, you've just taught your youngster that his resistance is permissible, in fact, rewarded. Down the road, this will make life difficult for you, your farrier, and your veterinarian.

• Your first session with the newborn is important, but equally so are your daily sessions in the days, weeks, and months to follow. These reinforce the lessons and deepen the bond. As time goes by, and you introduce new activities, you'll be well on your way to creating the partnership of your dreams.

PART THREE

RESOURCE GUIDE

FARMS & TRAINING FACILITIES

Arabians Ltd.
Jim and Judy Sirbasku
Waco, Texas
254-714-1803
arabiansltd@arabiansltd.com
www.arabiansltd.com

Babcock Ranch
Jim Babcock, Owner
Khris Crowe, DVM, MS, PC,
    Breeding Manager
Carlton Crowe, Ranch Manager
Valley View, Texas
940-665-7961
bqhoffice@nortexinfo.net
www.babcockranch.com

**Ball Quarter Horses and Stallion
    Station**
Margo, Wayne, and Tom Ball
Fort Collins, Colorado
970-484-4148
http://ballquarterhorses.com

**Bath Brothers Ranch/Randy Dunn
    Quarter Horses**
Randy Dunn
Laramie, Wyoming
307-742-4669
www.cometothesource.com/dunn.html

Buckshot Farms
Cory Vokoun
Roca, Nebraska
www.buckshotfarms.com

Cedar Grove Farm
Dr. Mike and Kathy Hartong
Peacham, Vermont
Jhartong@together.net
www.rockymountainhorsevermont.com

Char-O-Lot Ranch
Doug and Sue Schembri
Myckka City, Florida
941-322-1882
info@charolotranch.com
www.charolotranch.com

Crown Morgans
Nancy Eidam
Hermiston, Oregon
541-922-5484

**Down the Rail Performance
    Prospects**
Joe and Suzy Jeane
Valley View, Texas
940-668-8553
joejeane@msn.com
www.downtherail.com

Druid Oak Arabians
Jill & Joe Zamowski
12150 Olde South Lane
McCalla, Alabama 35111

Eleanor's Arabians
Eleanor Hamilton
Rogers, Minnesota
763-767-1381
800-328-9923
h.hamilton@microcontrol.com
www.eleanorsarabians.com

El Miladi Arabian Stud
Cynthia Culbertson
Carrizozo, New Mexico
505-648-2612
elmiladi@tularosa.net

Evergreen Arabians
Harold and Elizabeth Green
Los Olivos, California
805-693-9825
www.evergreenarabians.com

Fire Run Farm
Kurt and Teri Rumens
Snohomish, Washington
425-481-9481
kurt.rumens@gte.net
www.firerunfarm.com

Fullerton Training & Management, Inc.
Clint Fullerton
Oak Grove, Missouri
816-564-7071
Fullertonhorse@aol.com
www.fullertonmanagement.com

Imperial Egyptian Stud
Barbara Griffith
Parkton, Maryland
410-329-6380
IESArabs@aol.com
www.ImperialEgyptianStud.com

Kebra Ranch
Dr. Kim and Debra Sloan
Newfoundland, New Jersey
973-697-2020
info@kebra.com
www.kebra.com

Maritime Morgans
Julie Bair
Waterford, Pennsylvania
maritimemorgans@velocity.net
www.maritimemorgans.com

McQuay Stables
Tim McQuay, Owner
Billy J. Powers, Breeding Manager
Tioga, Texas
940-437-2470
mcquaystables@direcway.com
www.mcquaystables.com

Myers Horse Farms, Inc.
Ann Myers
Ashland, Ohio
419-289-0980
www.ZipsChocolateChip.com

Paradise Arabians
Gary and Wanda Kenworthy
Dalton, Georgia
706-397-9950
garyk@paradisearabians.com
www.paradisearabians.com

Poetry In Motion Arabians, Inc.
Steven and Zita Strother
Fresno, California
559-497-2100
poetryinmotion@mindspring.com
www.poetryinmotionarabians.com

Rancho Bulakenyo
Drs. Jody and Karen Cruz
Los Osos, California
805-534-1391
Richtermh@aol.com
www.ranchobulakenyo.com

Don Severa
Templeton, California
805-239-1019
dasevera@aol.com

Siaset Farm
Whit & Kathy Byers
Aubrey, Texas
940-365-2424

Ken Siefer Training
Ken Siefer
Sequim, Washington
360-582-0869

Silver Maple Farm
Henry and Christie Metz
Santa Ynez, California
805-686-5252
info@smfarabs.com
www.smfarabs.com

Source Arabians International
Vaughn and Victoria Snelgrove
Ontario, Canada
800-461-2899
SourceArabians@execulink.com
www.SourceArabians.com

Swalde Quarter Horses
Marilyn and Rich Swalde
Longmont, Colorado
303-652-2887
RSwalde@aol.com
Swaldequarterhorses.com

Tuscani Arabians
Stuart and Brenda Schuettpelz
Niles, Michigan
TUSCAN2@msn.com
www.tuscaniarabians.com

Varian Arabians
Sheila Varian
Arroyo Grande, California
805-489-5802
varianarab@aol.com
www.varianarabians.com

Windhorse Farm
Ron and Mila Hart
Santa Ynez, California
805-693-9458
rhart50538@aol.com
www.emanor.com

Winsome, Etc. Miniatures
Jane Taylor
Monroe, Washington
360-794-1241
winsomeetc@yahoo.com
www.winsomeetc.com

George Z Training Center
George Zbyszewski
Auburn, Washington
253-735-0357
GeorgeZTraining@aol.com

Veterinarians & Reproductive Specialists

American College of
  Theriogenologists
Montgomery, Alabama
334-395-4666
www.theriogenology.org

Whit Byers & Erin Bishop
Select Breeders Southwest, Inc.
Aubrey, Texas
940-365-2467
info@SelectBreederssw.com
www.SelectBreedersService.com

Whit Byers & Larry Shoemaker
Breeders Choice, LLC
Aubrey, Texas
940-365-2231
info@BreedersChoiceonline.com
www.BreedersChoiceOnline.com

Jill (Thayer) Cook, DVM
Royal Vista Equine
Fort Collins, Colorado
970-226-4747
www.royalvistaequine.com

Barb Crabbe, DVM
Jennifer Posey, DVM
Pacific Crest Sporthorse
Oregon City, Oregon
503-632-6336

Robert Foss, DVM
Equine Medical Services, Inc.
Columbia, Missouri
573-443-4414
equinemedical@aol.com
www.equmed.com

Heidi Immegart, DVM, MS, PhD,
  Diplomate, The American
  College of Theriogenologists
Veterinary Reproductive Specialists,
  Ltd.
Powell, Ohio
740-965-9433

Robert M. Miller, DVM
Robert M. Miller Communications
Truckee, California
530-582-4099
www.robertMmiller.com

Robert Morbray, DVM
Port Angeles, Washington
360-452-8978

Rood & Riddle Equine Hospital
Lexington, Kentucky
859-233-0371
rreh@roodandriddle.com
www.roodandriddle.com

Dave Sauter, DVM
Kulshan Veterinary Hospital
Lynden, Washington
360-354-5095
DrKulshan@msn.com
www.drkulshan.com

CONTRIBUTING PHOTOGRAPHERS

Richard T. Bryant
Richard T. Bryant Photography
Carrizozo, New Mexico
505-648-5888
richard.t.bryant@tularosa.net
www.richardtbryant.com

Randi Clark
Randi Clark Photography
Waco, Texas
254-752-5755
randiclark@hot.rr.com

Jay Goss
Jay Goss Photography
Monroe, Washington
360-799-2491
info@jaygoss.com
www.jaygoss.com

Mike Hartong
Cedar Grove Farm
Peacham, Vermont
Jhartong@together.net
www.rockymountainhorsevermont.com

Cappy Jackson
Cappy Jackson Photos
Sparks, Maryland
410-472-3670
cappyphotos@earthlink.net
www.cappyjackson.com

Darryl Larson
Darryl Larson Photography
Mount Dora, Florida
352-267-5549
Vids4U@aol.com

Heidi Nyland
The Whole Picture
Hilliard, Ohio
303-903-1349
wholepicture@wholepicture.org
www.wholepicture.org

Don Severa
Templeton, California
805-239-1019
dasevera@aol.com

Zita Strother
Strother Photography
Fresno, California
559-497-2100
Poetryinmotion@mindspring.com
www.imagesbyzita.com

Robert Vavra
www.robertvavra.com

Stuart Vesty
Vesty Photography
Aurora, Ohio
330-995-4800
stu@vesty.com
www.vesty.com

REGISTRIES & ASSOCIATIONS

American Association of Equine
Practitioners
Lexington, Kentucky
859-233-0147
www.aaep.org

American Buckskin Registry
Association, Inc.
Redding, California
530-223-1420
www.americanbuckskin.org

American Horse Council
Washington, DC
202-296-4031
ahc@horsecouncil.org
www.horsecouncil.org

American Miniature Horse
Association, Inc.
Alvarado, Texas
817-783-5600
information@amha.com
www.amha.com

American Miniature Horse Registry
Morton, Illinois
309-263-4044
www.shetlandminiature.com

American Morgan Horse
Association, Inc.
Shelburne, Vermont
802-985-4944
info@morganhorse.com
www.morganhorse.com

American Paint Horse Association
Fort Worth, Texas
817-834-2742
www.apha.com

American Quarter Horse
Association
Amarillo, Texas
806-376-4811
www.aqha.com

American Saddlebred Horse
Association
Lexington, Kentucky
859-259-2742
saddlebred@asha.net
www.saddlebred.com

American Warmblood Registry, Inc.
Royal Palm Beach, Florida
209-245-3565
americanwarmblood@aol.com
www.americanwarmblood.com

Appaloosa Horse Club, Inc.
Moscow, Idaho
208-882-5578
aphc@appaloosa.com
www.appaloosa.com

Arabian Horse Association
Aurora, Colorado
303-696-4500
www.arabianhorses.org

Arabian Reining Horse Association
Eleanor Hamilton, president
800-328-9923
h.hamilton@microcontrol.com
www.arha.net

Federation of North American
Sport Horse Registries
Lexington, Kentucky
859-255-4141
ahsoffice@aol.com

International Buckskin Horse
Association
Shelby, Indiana
219-552-1013
ibha@netnitco.net
www.ibha.net

The Jockey Club
Lexington, Kentucky
859-224-2700
www.jockeyclub.com

Missouri Fox Trotting Horse Breed
Association, Inc.
Ava, Missouri
417-683-2468
foxtrot@getgoin.net
www.mfthba.com

National Cutting Horse Association
Fort Worth, Texas
817-244-6188
www.nchacutting.com

National Pinto Horse Registry
Oxford, New York
607-334-4964
nphr@frontiernet.net
www.ascent.net/nphr

National Reined Cow Horse
Association
Byars, Oklahoma
580-759-4949
nrcha@brightok.net
www.nrcha.com

National Reining Horse Association
Oklahoma City, Oklahoma
405-946-7400
www.nrha.com

National Snaffle Bit Association
Tulsa, Oklahoma
918-270-1469
www.nsba.com

National Walking Horse
Association
Whitesboro, Texas
903-564-3747
www.nwha.com

Palomino Horse Association
Dornsife, Pennsylvania
570-758-3067
www.palominohorseassoc.com

Palomino Horse Breeders of
America
Tulsa, Oklahoma
918-438-1234
yellahorses@aol.com
www.palominohba.com

Paso Fino Horse Association, Inc.
Plant City, Florida
813-719-7777
www.pfha.org

Performance Horse Registry
Lexington, Kentucky
859-258-2472
phr@equestrian.org
www.phr.com

Peruvian Paso Horse Registry of
North America
Santa Rosa, California
707-579-4394
info@pphrna.org
www.pphrna.org

Pinto Horse Association of
America, Inc.
Fort Worth, Texas
817-336-7842
pinto@pinto.org
www.pinto.org

Pony of the Americas Club, Inc.
Indianapolis, Indiana
317-788-0107
www.poac.net

The Pyramid Society
Lexington, Kentucky
859-231-0771
info@PyramidSociety.org
www.PyramidSociety.org

Rocky Mountain Horse Association
Mount Olivet, Kentucky
606-724-2354
www.rmhorse.com

Tennessee Walking Horse Breeders'
and Exhibitors' Association
Lewisburg, Tennessee
800-359-1574; 931-359-1574
www.twhbea.com

United States Dressage Federation
Lexington, Kentucky
859-971-2277
usdressage@usdf.org
www.usdf.org

(courtesy of American Paint Horse Association)

Acknowledgments

My deep appreciation goes to our veterinarian contributors, reproductive specialists, breeding managers, trainers, and other consultants who gave so freely of their time and expertise. Their commitment to the horse and fellow horsepeople is without equal.

I thank each and every one of our contributing photographers, who generously provided inspiring images of mares, foals, and stallions captured with singular talent, infinite patience, a bit of serendipity, and an expert eye.

And thanks to all those who shared their breeding experiences so our brave readers will know they aren't alone in the joys—and heartbreaks—that go hand-in-hand with bringing a healthy and beautiful foal into the world.

Contact information for each of these valuable contributors is listed in the resource guide. Don't miss it.

I'd also like to express profound gratitude to Heidi Nyland and Jennifer Paulson for their research and journalistic assistance, without which this book simply wouldn't have been possible.

And finally, many thanks to Steven D. Price, our editor, for giving us a chance.

—*René E. Riley*

I would like to echo my heartfelt appreciation to the fine folks René has already thanked so well. I've learned much from them—our generous collaborators. I've laughed and cried as they shared stories about their horses, stories that I'll never forget.

While inspiration has come from many sources, I must offer my special thanks to a friend whose love for horses knows no bounds: Robert Vavra. How so much relentless, creative genius can reside in one individual, I do not know, but am forever grateful that it does.

Particular thanks to Sheila Varian, for her laughter and encouragement; and for breeding beautiful, useful horses for half a century. Hearty thanks to all of The Pyramid Society's horse breeders. Their passion, expertise, and horses enrich these pages greatly. Sincere thanks to Billy Powers, breeding manager *par excellence* at McQuay Stables.

And finally, thanks to my sage friend, horsewoman Cynthia Culbertson, for sharing an Arab proverb on breeding horses: *"A gold jewel cannot be made except from gold."* I pass it on to our readers—may your breeding experience be golden.

—*Honi Roberts*

(photo by Zita)

ABOUT THE AUTHORS

René E. Riley is a lifelong horsewoman with sixteen years' experience in the equine-publishing field. While executive editor of *Horse & Rider* magazine, the publication captured honorable mention in the American Horse Publication's General Excellence category. She's currently the editor of *The Trail Rider* magazine and *Equine Veterinary Management,* a business journal for equine veterinarians. She resides in Evergreen, Colorado.

Honi Roberts is an award-winning writer and photographer whose work has appeared in books, newspapers, and leading national equine publications, including *Horse & Rider, The Trail Rider, Performance Horse,* the National Reining Horse Association's *Reiner,* and *The Arabian Horse Times.* She lives in Washington State with her three Arabian mares, two dogs, and one cat.

INDEX